Humans Think.
Animals Feel.

Finding Common Ground
Between You
and Your Animal Friends

Humans Think.
Animals Feel.

Finding Common Ground
Between You
and Your Animal Friends

Patty Rayman

GRAY**CAT**

Copyright ©2017 Patty Rayman

All rights reserved.

No part of this publication may be reproduced, stored in a retrieval system, or transmitted in any form or by any means, electronic, mechanical, photocopying, recording, or otherwise, without written permission of the publisher.

Published in the United States by
Gray Cat LLC

ISBN: 978-0-9993957-0-7

Library of Congress Control Number: 2017916016

Book cover design by: Michelle Rayner, Cosmic Design

Interior design by: Katie Mullaly, Surrogate Press™

To Cotton, my greatest teacher.

I am still learning.

Table of Contents

Table of Contents vii

Acknowledgements 1

Introduction 3
    Moving Energy Down and Up 10
    Left and Right Brain Breathing 11
    Automatic Writing 13

Chapter One: Brains and Thinking 16
    Thinking and Feeling Like an Animal 24

Chapter Two: Awareness and Focus 27
    Physical Awareness 28
    Mental Awareness 37
    Emotional Awareness 46
    Thinking About Emotion 54

Chapter Three: Using Some of Your Best Skills 59
    Visualization 61
    Creating Expectations 67
    Establishing Boundaries 71
    Pushback 80

Chapter Four: Changing Behavior 82
    Approval and Disapproval 86
    What Animals Want 92

Chapter Five: Practical Examples 95
    Inappropriate Elimination 95
    Separation Anxiety 102
    Stop Barking 109
    Ignore.. 113
    Cats... 119
    Moving 127
    Missing Animals 135

Chapter Six: Food and Exercise 142
    Ingredients to Avoid 146
    Making Good Choices... 147
    Changing Their Diet 150

Conclusion 158

About the Author 160

Acknowledgements

Many people contribute to the creation of a book. First and foremost, I would like to thank all of the people who trusted a random person they found on the Internet for help and advice about their animals. I love my clients and I have learned so much from them. I have worked with people from all over the world, from every walk of life. No matter what they do for a living or where they live, the respect, love and devotion they have for their animals is boundless. I have worked with some clients for years and have watched their animals grow up, grow old and pass on. Thank you for letting me share these intimate moments with you. I feel like my clients are family even though I have never met many of you in person.

Through the years, people have encouraged me to share what I've learned in the form of a book. The great crew at Lifelong Learning at the University of Utah gave me the opportunity to "preach what I practice" on the many occasions I taught classes. Interacting with students helped me develop the exercises in this book. They also asked great questions and sparked many interesting conversations.

For the actual production of the book, I would like to sing the praises of Stacy Dymalski, Katie Mullaly and Michelle Rayner who helped me present this information to a much wider audience.

Also thanks to my early readers Sarah Dalling, Meggin Weinandt and Lori Pugh who suffered through lengthy and disorganized rough drafts. Writing a book is not easy and reading a half-finished one is not easy, either.

This book details how to develop balanced relationships with your animals. Once we understand how to think like them, we can expand our basic communication into something much more significant. I have learned more from animals about the meaning of life, the power of love and how to express joy than from any human teacher. I have also learned what it means to live with grace, overcome adversity and die with dignity. I look forward to spending the rest of my life working with animals and the people that love them. Every animal I have worked with has touched my heart in some way and I am grateful for the opportunity to help them.

I want to reference a few books that have shaped my thinking and helped me become a better animal communicator. I am a voracious reader and take inspiration from many sources, but *Excuse Me, Your Life is Waiting* by Lynn Grabhorn in particular helped me refine my ability to share strong emotions with animals. *Ask and It Is Given*, by Esther and Jerry Hicks provided the model for the Emotional Staircase. It is derived from their Emotional Ladder exercise but because animals can't climb ladders very well, it made more sense to have them going up and down stairs. Stacy Dymalski's book *The Memoir Midwife, Nine Steps to Self-publishing Your Book* was my Bible and got me through the rather long process of creating an actual book from piles of scribbled notes.

I especially want to thank you, the reader for taking time out of your busy life to improve your relationship with your animals. Give them all a good belly rub for me. You are making their lives happier and healthier. Learning to work with animals also helps you become more mindful and compassionate. The world can use more of that energy right now. Time spent with animals is never wasted.

Patty Rayman

Introduction

I have been a professional Animal Communicator for over twenty years and I can tell you no one calls a Pet Psychic when their animal is happy and healthy. People call me to help them solve problems. Animals enrich our lives in many ways, but actually living with them is not always easy. They can be expensive, time-consuming and a lot of the tasks associated with them are rather thankless, like scooping litter boxes or cleaning dog hair off the couch. We share a deep bond with our animal companions, but people often become frustrated when their animals exhibit undesirable behaviors. Animals can be *very* intent on getting what they want and are willing to use all of their abilities to get it. Some people describe their relationship with their dog, cat or horse as the most emotionally challenging aspect of their life. Animals get confused when they don't get clear information from the people around them. This leads to communication breakdowns and stress for both parties. You can use some of your best human thinking skills to change these important relationships for the better, avoiding some of the most common human-animal challenges that I work with.

The animals that share your life may influence everything from where you live, the vehicle you drive and choices you make about your career. In exchange, animals give us huge amounts of love, comfort and joy. When you give them information in ways they understand, you are better able to provide them the mental and emotional connection that they desire. Successful communication almost always reduces conflict and adds to the emotional well-being of both partners. You spend a lot of time, energy and money on your animal companions, so take this opportunity to develop the most enriching and satisfying relationships possible.

Some of the benefits of improving your communication skills include, but certainly are not limited to, the following:

- Better awareness and control of your emotions
- Consciously choosing to experience positive feelings in a given situation
- Experiencing fewer negative emotions over all

There are no bad animals, but I have helped many people work through bad animal behavior and dysfunctional patterns. I want to help *you* solve conflicts and reduce daily frustrations so you can concentrate on the deeper, more satisfying parts of your relationships. If you love animals, you already have the skills you need to effectively change their behavior. I believe that communicating with animals is a natural ability that many people share and is something that can be developed. This is not a training method for animals or about forcing them to submit to your will. This book details a way to compassionately change your animal's behavior by using your best mental and emotional abilities. You will learn how to get your animal to want to work with you instead of against you.

I have worked mostly with dogs, cats and horses but have done readings for just about every type of animal somebody loves. These techniques work with all types of animals (even cats). This book will not teach you how to intuitively communicate with animals, but it will help you understand your physical, mental and emotional contributions to the specific

Introduction

animal behaviors that negatively impact your relationship. My second book, *Humans Think, Animals Feel, Part 2*, will detail the more psychic aspects of animal communication like asking animals questions and interpreting their answers.

Animals have always been my friends. I was born with the ability to communicate with them and have been doing so all my life. I was kind of a weird kid and not very social with people. I was much more comfortable being around animals. I was probably ten before I figured out that other people didn't understand them the way I did. I thought everyone knew that you talked to humans in words and animals in pictures and I was quite surprised to find out otherwise. I learned pretty quickly to not talk about what the animals were telling me. Because my parents didn't ask, they couldn't disapprove of the fact that I was having conversations with animals and they couldn't say it was "just my imagination." I believe that everyone is born psychic, but unfortunately, by the time kids are about four, we disapprove of their visions and society puts limits on their dreams.

Gradually, this ability faded into the background and lay dormant for a number of years. I didn't do much with it until I was in college and some well-meaning, but clueless, friends took in a stray kitten on a rainy Saturday night. They called and said I had to take the cat because their landlord wouldn't let them keep it. I don't often hear the animal's *voice*, but I have always been able to receive their mental pictures and feel the associated emotions. After I fed the little ball of fluff, I was quite surprised when I distinctly heard him say, "My name is Cotton. If you let me live out my natural life span, I will help you develop your gifts."

I agreed to this unusual proposition and am very glad I did. Cotton lived to be twenty years old and in his own quiet way taught me how to dialog with animals and translate their pictures into words for people. He was my mentor and my guide. Because of him, I learned how to think like an animal and I can teach you how to do this, too.

You may have noticed that I don't use the words 'pets' and 'owners' to refer to animals and the people who love them. I truly appreciate how important animals are to us and I am deliberate with the words I choose to describe the heart-felt connection we have with them. I like to bake and I have a sourdough starter. I think of it as a pet. I feed it and it is useful to me, but it is not an important part of my life. To me, ownership is a very unequal relationship; the thing being owned has less value than the owner. I *own* my cat in a very abstract way; my information is on her microchip and I am responsible for her, but we co-create our partnership.

We can choose to see animals as objects, property or as a way to serve our emotional needs. In truth, animals are our partners, our friends and our teachers. We share our lives with them. They are unique individuals and they have their own agendas. They are the subject of their lives and deserve to be treated as the intelligent, emotionally responsive beings they are. Our relationships with animals have much more resonance than the words *pet* and *owner* imply.

My cat is so much more than a pet. Her name is Monster and she is a little different. She was found as a young orphan and was placed with a mother cat that had slightly younger babies at the shelter. The mother got distemper and all of the kittens got it, too. Monster was the only survivor. Distemper causes neurological problems and Monster went from being a sweet, snuggly baby to being an aggressive biter. A friend of mine calls her the Land Piranha. She was taken in by a family who was very involved in animal rescue and

Introduction

had raised many dogs and cats. They called me to do a reading with her because they could not figure her out. Even as a young kitten she would hunt the other cats in the house and get them treed on top of the refrigerator. The other cats, the dogs and even the people were terrified of her and she spent most of her time in a large cage. I helped them develop a plan to maintain relative harmony by letting her live by herself. I was working at an independent pet food store and we tried Monster as our shop cat. This was a rather spectacular failure because she bit a customer, so she went back to her foster family.

Animals get with the right people and somehow she clawed her way into my heart. I moved to another state and for reasons I still don't understand, one day I picked up the phone and called Monster's foster family. She was supposed to be my cat. The first night I had her, she bit me in the face while I was asleep. Her first two weeks with me were pretty much a bloodbath. She would charge me like a wild animal and I had bites and scratches all over my arms and face. She figured out that my hands are bony and would launch herself at my much meatier shoulder. I seriously considered taking her back. I believe that if you say, "I love you" to an animal you have made a commitment to them, so I screwed my courage to the sticking place, bought a big box of bandages and decided to keep her.

I had no idea how to change a half-crazed fiend into a domesticated companion, but I had no other choice than to try. I started by getting her used to being touched. I would feed her yummy canned food and stroke her sides and back while I told her what a good cat she was. I didn't know cats could growl while they were eating, but she did. We slowly progressed to a more peaceful coexistence. It took me nine months to touch her head. I had to teach her how to not bite (I detail this in a later chapter). After about two and a half years, she was able to sit on my lap. I kept the expectation that she would become more normal and she did.

Monster made me practice what I preach and use all of my communication skills. I could have used intimidation or violence to 'break' her habits, but I chose to find other solutions to her extreme behaviors. Mindlessly picking her up like I would any other cat will result in a painful bite. I have to always be aware of how she feels physically and emotionally because being disconnected leads to bloodshed. My expectation about not getting bitten helped me develop behavioral boundaries that are enforced to this day. I had to practice in order to give her strong emotional corrections while using the least amount of physical force. There wasn't any magic involved in this, just a lot of awareness and persistence. Monster is unique and I never take her for granted. In some ways, she is a very good cat. She doesn't jump on the counters or scratch my furniture and she has never had an accident outside of her litter box. I am very thankful for her good behavior. She is charming in her own way and I tell her she is the best cat on the planet.

I also don't use words like 'telepathy,' which sounds like something from a bad *Star Trek* episode. There is nothing mystical about this technique. It is a way for you to use your highly developed human brain to create the partnership that works for you and your animal. My relationship with Monster doesn't look like anyone else's, it is unique to us. The point is, we can live together in relative harmony in spite of our rough beginning. You have the ability to change your thinking and change your experience with your animals.

Introduction

Even difficult relationships can improve and behaviors that have gone on for years can be changed.

The first part of this book explains some of the differences in how humans and animal think. Humans are verbal, logical and often preoccupied with the past or the future. Animals, however, think in pictures, are emotionally aware and live in the present. Our brains are different, but we can choose to think like animals and this ability is essential in getting them to cooperate with us.

The second part of the book gives some practical examples of how to apply these techniques in real life situations. These are the behaviors that people most often call me about and this section will empower you to make effective changes. At the end is a chapter about food. How and what you feed your animal has a huge impact on their quality of life and this section gives you some information to make healthy choices for them.

Life is experiential and we learn when we try new things. There is no right or wrong way to explore your connection with animals, but developing your innate abilities is like learning a new language and you will have to practice. Anyone who has cultivated any kind of skill has had to practice. Athletes practice, musicians practice, even poker players practice. Often the more gifted someone is, the more they practice to refine their talents. The more you practice thinking like an animal, the easier it will be to reduce conflict and improve your relationship.

I have taught Animal Communication classes and workshops for many years and have developed several exercises to help people connect with their animal communication abilities. These exercises are throughout the book and are indicated by **bold type**. They are simple and don't require special preparation. Do the exercises with an open mind; they work for me and the people who have taken my classes. Try all of them at least once and find the ones that work the best for you. Below are the three exercises I refer to the most often. These are the fundamental skills in communicating with animals and I feel it is important to become proficient with them.

As you explore your natural ability to communicate with animals, I suggest keeping a journal. You are conducting behavioral experiments, so record observations like a scientist. Write about your goals, the actions you plan to take and record the results of your experiments. What other questions came up? What is the next step? Writing down the answers to these questions will help you refine your technique and work through complex behavior patterns. It is rewarding to review these notes and acknowledge how much progress you have made. When Monster sits on my lap purring, it is very gratifying to remember how far our partnership has come.

Moving Energy Down and Up

This exercise is a great way to check in with yourself by bringing awareness to your body and your mind into the present moment. Use these images or any others that you like. The important thing is to feel the different ways energy moves through you. Imagine that you have a trap door on the top of your head. Picture that little door swinging open. Pretend you are standing under a shower and a slow trickle of warm water is pouring through the open door. The water flows down through your head, your throat, into your chest, through your arms, your belly and into your legs. Allow your body to soften. Feel energy moving through every part of you. Feel it flow out your feet into the Earth.

Open up the tap and let more energy flow through the top of your head, through your body and into the Earth. Feel the flow increase until you are standing under a waterfall. Let that energy wash through you, washing away doubts and worries. Feel the Earth absorb everything that that you send into her.

Now imagine you are a large tree. You have a leafy canopy that extends up into the sky, feeling the sun and the wind. You have a sturdy trunk and roots that go deep into the ground. Feel how the Earth cradles and supports your roots. Imagine your roots pulling energy up from the ground, like sucking water up through a straw. Feel the energy rising slowly and steadily up your body. Feel it move into your head. Feel that energy shoot out of your head like a fountain.

Can you feel the difference between energy flowing down and up? If you can feel this subtle difference, feeling the difference between two emotions will be easy. If you didn't feel anything, that's okay, pretend that you did. It may be easier to do this exercise standing on the ground or sitting near a tree. Keep practicing. This exercise helps bring you into the present and is a useful way to reduce stress.

Connecting with your energy and checking in with yourself physically, mentally and emotionally is essential when working with animals. This exercise (or any other form of mindfulness that you practice) helps you get out of your own way and focus on solving the problem instead of making it worse.

Left and Right Brain Breathing

The left side of the human brain is the logical, reasoning brain. It is responsible for symbolic thinking and active when you read or understand speech. The right side of the brain is much more visual and emotionally perceptive. These brain functions are not as localized as once thought, but this generalization is still useful. Choosing to activate your right brain allows you to think like an animal and make a connection with them.

I do this exercise every day and it is the most important skill to master if you want to effectively change your animal's behavior. This easy breathing practice helps you choose which part of your brain you want to use in a given situation. Sit in a chair, relaxed, with your feet flat on the floor. Close your eyes. With one or two fingers, block your left nostril and take five or six deep, slow breaths. Try not to think about anything in particular, just relax and breathe deeply. Notice how you feel after doing this. Are you alert and thinking more clearly? Do you have an urge to work on a spreadsheet? This is your left brain and it helps you focus on detail oriented tasks.

Now block your right nostril and take several deep breaths. Compare how you feel now with how you felt after activating your left brain. Notice if the voice in your head seems more subdued. The right brain is less verbal than the left brain. People describe this as an almost dreamlike state. Dreams are visual and the stories are often emotional. The stories have a weird kind of certainty to them. Even though your mother may appear as a giraffe, you know who she is and understand what she is saying to you. This type of knowing is similar to how I feel when I am receiving images and emotions from an animal.

Your brain is essentially cross wired; the left side of the brain controls the right side of the body and the right side of the brain controls the left side. That is why you **block your right nostril to activate your right brain**. Obviously, when you have a cold and can't breathe through your nose at all, that is not a good time to practice this exercise. Some people argue that breathing is breathing and it doesn't matter how the air enters your respiratory system. Your body and your mind are connected in infinite ways and what you do with one influences the other. This exercise is based on a Kundalini yoga practice that is several thousand years old, so I believe it has some validity. Choose to embrace your ability to communicate with animals instead of setting up roadblocks for yourself.

Use this breathing technique to shift into your right brain. Two things are important about this exercise. The first is experiencing how the right brain thinks. This is how you create the visual stories you will use to change your animal's behavior. The second is becoming consciously aware of the shift from the left brain to the right brain. Keep practicing until you can feel this difference.

Automatic Writing

Automatic Writing is a very useful tool to help clarify your emotions around any situation. Emotions tend to cloud our perceptions. Clear thinking is important for creating a plan of action to change a behavior. It is hard to put emotions into words, especially concerning relationships. This technique taps into the right brain and gives undefined emotions a constructive outlet. Our relationships with animals often generate both positive and negative emotions and Automatic Writing is an effective way to sort them out.

Writing by hand is a different experience than writing with a keyboard and uses another part of the brain. Sit down in a quiet place with a pen or pencil and a blank piece of paper. Block your right nostril and take a few deep breaths, connecting to your right brain. Set a timer for five minutes. Close your eyes and start writing. Yes, you read that correctly. You are going to write with your eyes closed. Your third grade teacher is not here and you won't be graded on this. Penmanship and staying within the lines DOES NOT count! What does count is expressing how you feel. The whole point is to not look at what you are writing.

The only "rules" are to keep your eyes closed and write until the timer goes off. You will probably start writing in semi-neat rows. As you get into it, the writing becomes looser and less constrained. Allow all of your feelings to come out on to that paper. Write and write and write. Rotate the paper, flip it over, just keep writing and keep your eyes closed. When the timer goes off, just look at the paper, don't try to read it. Look at the power of the words, noticing any that jump out or are repeated several times. This is how you really feel about the situation. This exercise is more about the process than about the product, so throw the paper away when finished. Many people find this very cathartic.

I don't do this exercise every day, but it is very useful for sorting out conflicting emotions. I find it invaluable when I feel 51% positive emotions and 49% negative emotions about something and am unable to take action. I wrote about my relationship with Monster (several times) when I was deciding to keep her. I have used Automatic Writing to sort through complex emotions around moving, changing jobs or staying in difficult human relationships. This exercise only takes a few minutes to do but has considerable payoffs in cutting through emotional static.

When I teach this exercise in classes it is fascinating to watch the emotion play out on people's faces while they write. Automatic Writing can bring up strong emotions, often those that exist at a subconscious level. We are emotional beings and giving deep emotions a voice will help get you out of reactive cycles in your relationships. Get comfortable with this technique; it is an important tool for working through specific behavior problems. As you are starting out, write about something positive. Here are a few sample topics:

- Describe what you love about your animal
- Explain why you share your life with your animal
- Recall how you felt when they were babies or when you first met them
- Write a love letter to each of your animals, living or passed on

Genetics, temperament and past experience (yours and theirs) influence your relationships with animals in ways you can't control. However, you can control your actions, thoughts and feelings. The better you understand your physical, mental and emotional interactions, the more you can modify your behavior to influence theirs. When you change the input in any relationship, the output also changes. No behavior exists in a vacuum and these exercises will help you become aware of how you contribute to the relationship. You already have the skills you need to create peaceful coexistence. Let me show you how to use them in new ways.

Chapter One:
Brains and Thinking

Before we get into the nuts and bolts of relationship building, it is important to understand how animals think. You can think like your dog, cat or horse, but she cannot think like you. Our animal companions are very much like us; we are all made of dust, water and a little cosmic spark. We breathe the same air and feel the same pull of gravity on our bodies, but animals and humans think differently. We can communicate more effectively and approach relationships in a less reactive way by understanding some of these differences. This is partly due to brain anatomy. Brains are incredibly complex and there are many regions that carry out cognitive functions, so this is a very general overview of some important parts of our brains.

The Brainstem

Humans have three distinct, vertically stacked brain regions, the brainstem, the limbic brain and the neocortex. The oldest part of the brain is the brainstem, which sits on top of the spinal cord. It regulates things like breathing, heart rate, body temperature and automatic reflexes. The brainstem helps you take immediate action, like in a fight or flight situation. This region is also called the *reptile brain* because it is not emotionally responsive. I have worked with reptiles and they are beautiful and very interesting, but they are not like mammals. They have individual personalities and can certainly tell the difference between what feels good to them and what doesn't, but I have never felt love or grati-

Chapter One: Brains and Thinking

tude from a reptile. They can recognize people and respond to individuals in their environment. However, they see you as a supplier; you give them light, warmth and food, but they cannot return the love you give them.

I did a reading for a client who had a variety of animals, dogs, cats and a large iguana named Bowie. He was about three feet long and had free run of the house. He lived in an interesting environment, had lots of interaction with other animals and people and had plenty of room to move around. She called a few months later because Bowie escaped. Iguanas can run very fast for short distances, which he did, right across the yard and up into the trees! It was summer and he basically went native because he was a wild animal.

This is a perfect example of the reptile brain in action. Bowie had no love or attachment for his people and was not interested in going home. I was able to connect with him, but I couldn't tell him the house would be a better place to live or appeal to him about how much his people missed him, like I would with a dog or cat. There was nothing I could tell him to make him give up what he had, because all of his needs were being met and he had no connection to his home or people.

The woman called back the following October. There had been a cold snap and Bowie fell out of a neighbor's tree, stiff as a board. He was none the worse for wear for having lived outside for several months. After he thawed out, I visited with him and he showed me pictures of eating fruit and stealing dog food. Many people chased him, but no one was able to catch him. He didn't miss his people and didn't try to find his way home, it was just chance that he ended up where he started.

The Limbic Brain

The next brain region wraps around the brainstem and is called the limbic brain. This is the part of the brain that is emotionally attentive. It enables vocal communication and the understanding of a variety of calls and sounds from within a species and other animals in the environment. The limbic brain allows humans and our companion animals to feel compassion and make emotional connections to others. This is how a mother bat can return from a night of eating insects to find her baby in a cave with millions of other bats and why your dog does the happy dance when you walk in the door. Animal thinking is dominated by the limbic brain and animals are much more emotional and reactive than humans.

Because of the limbic brain, mammals are able to engage in the totally nonsensical activity of play. Play shows an understanding of the intent of the other and is an important form of communication. When dogs play bow to each other (front legs extended on the ground and rear up, tail wagging) they are basically making a contract that says, "Let's play! I have no intention of hurting you, even though we will be doing the same actions that could lead to serious harm in another situation." Our domestic animals play all of their lives. Humans seem to be unique in our ability to forget how to engage each other in this way. Mammals and birds can even learn to play across species. However, you don't see snakes and alligators playing with each other.

I have a theory that dogs are drawn to other dogs that look like them in the face. Dogs don't know what they look like but they respond to a face that is similar to their mother's or their siblings'. Dogs have particularly strong bonds to their littermates and I have seen dogs that have been separated for years ecstatically greet their brothers or sisters. I was doing readings at a dog show when I observed an unusual encounter between a Belgian Shepherd and a Sheltie. Belgian Shepherds are large, athletic dogs who are often very assertive. Shelties are much smaller and tend to be protective of their people. Both dogs were male and as they walked towards each other, they started a staring contest. Instead of barking, lunging and trying to determine who was in charge, they both went down into play bows and started wagging their tails. The thing that was interesting is both dogs had solid black faces and upright ears. When they looked at each other, they saw a familiar face and decided to be friends rather than foes.

The Neocortex

The outermost part of the brain sets us apart from our companion animals. This is the neocortex and it gives humans the ability to think rationally, solve complex problems and communicate symbolically. Dogs and cats do have a neocortex, but ours is much more developed. Hunting animals need to solve problems every day or they go hungry. Social animals have more complex brains than those who don't live in groups because they need to exchange information with each other. Animals can definitely think and solve problems, but they can't think abstractly or metaphorically like humans can.

A good example of this is a reading I did for two Jack Russell Terriers. The house had a low deck in the back yard and there were rats living underneath it. The smaller dog would crawl under the deck and scare the rats out and the larger dog would kill them. They each had a role to play and they cooperated to achieve a goal. They were both very proud of the job they did protecting the house.

The neocortex carries out many types of advanced thinking, but our abilities to think about the past and future and understand a situation from another's perspective are the most essential for communicating with animals. This brain region is responsible for one of our most uniquely human attributes, the ability to think about thinking. We highly value intelligence and we have used our problem-solving and communication skills to completely shape this world. Humans are pretty conceited about our thinking abilities and we like to evaluate other animals in terms of ourselves.

Domestic animals are very intelligent, but not to the level of adult humans. As a rough approximation, a dog is like a two-year-old child and a cat is like an 18-month-old. This is not a direct comparison because human toddlers can't herd sheep or hunt mice, but more of a general idea. Dogs usually understand more words than cats, but I have worked with some very smart cats and some dogs that were not the sharpest tools in the shed. I don't know how horses compare to humans intelligence-wise; they are prey animals and we are predators, so we have different ways of solving problems. Herds can have very complex social dynamics, almost like soap operas. Some horses are very good at figuring out how gates and door latches work and are often expert escape artists. Just because animals don't think like us, it is a mistake to underestimate them.

What we consider intelligence varies dramatically by species, breed and individual. Working dogs often understand many words and are better at interpreting a pointing gesture than chimpanzees. I worked with a Border Collie named All-Star who was the smartest dog I have ever met. I knew he was pretty special when he started jumping up the

Chapter One: Brains and Thinking

stairs backwards. His person had taught him many tricks and one of his favorites was *Recycle*. The woman would give him the command and he would take an empty plastic bottle off the desk and put it in the bin. She made this more challenging by having two bottles on the desk, one that was empty and one that had an inch of water in it. All-Star would invariably choose the empty bottle. Most dogs (and many people) don't understand that word, let alone know what to do when they hear it. He not only understood the command, he seemed to have a concept of which bottle was appropriate to pick up.

Cats are basically furry little rocket scientists. They are excellent at determining speed and trajectory because they hunt small prey, which can change direction very quickly. Our complex human brains help us accurately throw things like rocks, spears and ballistic missiles. Cats can't throw anything except attitude, but they can launch their bodies very precisely through space. Cats are intelligent and trainable, but most people have never tried to train their cat. Once I succeeded in taming Monster, I thought it would be fun to teach her some tricks. She knows how to *sit pretty*, which is where she sits up on her haunches like a fat prairie dog and she can also jump on command. Her best trick is to come when I call her. I have better recall with my cat than many of my clients do with their dogs.

The Left and Right Brains

Fortunately for us, our neocortex is divided into two parts. The left half of the neocortex controls activities like speech, reasoning and numerical thinking. I refer to this as the **Big, Fat Human Brain** (BFHB) and it is great for doing things like reading, following a map or making complex plans for the future. But it tends to get us in trouble where animal communication is concerned. In a lot of ways, we are slaves to our logical, speech-oriented left brains. We think in words and tend to overlook other types of information that are available to us.

The right side of the brain is responsible for nonlinear functions like creativity, imagination and recognizing complex patterns. This part of the brain is great at thinking visually and interpreting emotion. Children rely heavily on their non-verbal and emotionally perceptive right brains before learning to speak. To effectively communicate with animals, you need to reconnect with these abilities and dust off some skills you may not have used for a while. In most adults, the right brain is quietly working in background, allowing the left brain to dominate your experience.

The left brain is in charge of your "To Do" list. Doing the **Left Brain Breathing Exercise** (blocking your left nostril) to consciously engage this part of your brain is very effective at three o'clock in the afternoon when you need to finish a project, but you really want to hit the vending machine to get a nice sugary snack or a cup of coffee. The left brain helps you focus on the future. The BFHB is chatty and likes to comment on everything that is going on. It is busy organizing thoughts and wondering/worrying about things that may or may not happen. If you gave voice to all of the verbal thoughts in your head, people would assume you were crazy and they would move away from you on the bus. Communicating with animals is, in a large part, about turning off this voice in your head.

The right part of the brain is not task-oriented or interested in your internal monologue. It is focused on the present. Thinking with the right brain helps disengage the BFHB, allowing you to think like your animals and connect with them in a genuine way. This type of awareness helps you move out of emotionally reactive cycles because you can see events from another's perspective and understand their motivations. Do the **Moving Energy Down and Up** and the **Right Brain Breathing** exercises to activate your right brain. This is your Being self. We are not Human Doings, so this is an important part of yourself to cultivate.

Because humans are so left brain biased, we often overlook what is happening around us. Animals are very discerning of their physical and emotional environment and respond to it in real time. When you bring your focus into the present, you can avoid getting into an emotional struggle with your animal, like when the dog won't get in the car and you are going to be late for your vet appointment. If you stop worrying about what might happen in the future, you can redirect your energy towards what you are doing, saying and feeling in the moment. Maybe you are giving your dog conflicting signals and he doesn't understand what you want. Taking a couple of deep breaths while blocking your right nostril helps you calm down and step out of an increasingly negative cycle.

When people get in emotional struggles with animals, the animal wins or the situation deteriorates and the human uses too much force. Dogs, cats and horses are single-minded about getting what they want in that moment. When you play the game of human emotion versus animal emotion, you have just disconnected most of your neocortex. Even worse, when you use physical strength against teeth or claws, you have also tossed out your limbic brain and are functioning in reptile mode. Your neck works hard to hold your head up, so you might as well use your brain to create a better relationship with your non-verbal and emotionally aware companion.

Thinking and Feeling Like an Animal

Animals think of humans in their own terms. They understand that humans are different from other types of animals, but to a dog's way of thinking, people are like super, magical dogs. We make things happen that impact them greatly. We turn on lights, we open doors and give them tasty things to eat. We take them with us in unbelievably exciting cars to new places with fascinating smells. People tend to overestimate the intelligence of their animals and underestimate their emotional sensitivity. There are huge parts of our lives of which they can't conceive. Your dog does not know what the "economy" is or why it would influence your life. A cat cannot even form the idea of a "boss" and horses do not understand "divorce." Animals are the main actors in their stories, the subjects of their own lives. We play a huge supporting role, but their lives are still all about them.

Animals can't compare themselves to others or to how they were in the past. The complex thought process of evaluating a current state and contrasting it to something that no longer exists is an example of how our BFHB works. A man called me because his dog was going blind. He wanted to know if the dog was distressed about losing his sight. The dog wasn't, that would be projecting his current state into the future, something dogs can't do. The dog would accept his declining vision without question and without remorse. He would never think that he was being punished or denied some of the joy that was due to him. His body and his mind would compensate for the loss of information and he would just go on being a dog. The dog was much more interested in exerting his dominance over the other dog in the house than about his declining vision. Animals have a wonderful ability

Chapter One: Brains and Thinking

to emphasize what is really important: food, water, comfort, social interaction and love. They let everything else slide.

Animals live in the present moment. They don't think about time the way we do; they don't have a biography. Telling your biography is like putting beads on a string. The beads go on in a particular order and the color, shape and size of a specific bead influences the choice of the beads that follow. The beads relate to each other, have patterns and are presented sequentially. Humans can trace ideas through their lifetime and make a narrative about how one particular event influenced others and draw a cause-and-effect relationship.

Animals' life stories are more like a cup of beads and there is no temporal order. The beads are emotional events in their lives, and they can remember them in detail, but they can't tell a sequential story. They don't understand "why" something happened but they can relate their feelings about it. When I communicate with an animal, I see the most emotional events from their life, positive and negative, which are essentially the shiniest beads in their cup.

I did a reading for a woman who was wounded in a drive-by shooting while holding her dog and she wanted to know what the dog remembered about it. All he could recall was falling and then visiting his momma when she was in a bed that he couldn't get on. He didn't understand that she was badly injured and in the hospital, he just knew how happy he was to see her. Animals think in pictures and emotions. If I ask an animal to show me an event that was not emotionally significant to them, they probably can't. If I ask you what you had for lunch last Tuesday, you are unlikely to remember unless it was exceptional in some way. Animals have no ability to think about events outside of their experience. If the dog hadn't been with her, he would have no memory of that tragic event at all.

One of the most striking differences between humans and animals is what we seek emotionally. Humans spend a lot of energy trying to avoid situations we find unpleasant; we move away from negative emotions. For example, embarrassment is a minor, slightly negative emotion, but we go to great lengths to not experience this feeling. In contrast, animals move towards positive emotions. They expect to experience joy every day; they seek it and spend their energy to create positive experiences. Some people can count the number of times they have experienced joy on one hand.

Animals are fundamentally optimistic. This is one reason I chose to be an animal communicator instead of a people psychic. I have never met a pessimistic dog. I have met fearful dogs, depressed dogs and grieving dogs, but not a pessimistic one. Even if a dog has walked around the same block every day for 12 years, he still looks forward to that walk with eager anticipation. He just knows something interesting is out there, waiting to be discovered. People see sameness and repetition because we compare our past experiences to the present. Animals experience life as it happens and focus on positive emotion. Humans often choose to suffer, even when given viable alternatives and will stay stuck in painful situations because they fear change or are concerned about what others might think. Animals strongly desire to be happy and healthy and will quickly let go of unpleasant emotions if you give them a better option.

In the chapter on Changing Behavior, you will learn how to use some of your advanced thinking skills and emotional attunement to help your animals move away from negative patterns. By working with their natural optimism, you can transform their behavior and create better relationships.

Chapter Two: Awareness and Focus

One of the most important aspects of animal communication is awareness. Awareness is about being in the present and consciously choosing what you do, say and feel. When you change your physical, mental or emotional contribution to any relationship, you redefine it. Humans think and animals feel. Your natural ability to think about thinking allows you to break negative emotional patterns with your animals. When you actively participate in your relationships instead of just going through the motions, you can create better outcomes in many situations. You can't change your partner, but you can control your responses to their behavior.

Animals have limited ways of interacting with us. They don't have thumbs and can't text, so they use their bodies, behaviors and sounds to express themselves. The physical aspect of your relationship involves how you touch them and how they touch you. The mental portion includes how you think and talk about your animal in particular and the relationship in general. Thoughts become words and words become attitudes and actions. The emotional part of your relationship is the most powerful and also the most problematic. Of course you love your animals, but their behavior can generate large amounts of stress and negative feelings. By becoming connected to your emotions and directing them in a focused way, you can change a difficult relationship into one that is mutually satisfying for everyone involved. I used clearly defined emotions to change Monster's behavior and this will work with your animals as well.

Physical Awareness

Our physical relationship with animals is immediate and the easiest way to connect with them. We love to look at animals, touch them and in some cases, listen to them. We enjoy watching them move and experience the world. They use all of their physical senses all the time and don't classify and compartmentalize physical information, they just respond to it. Animals don't make a distinction between smell, sight and hearing the way we do. Their senses are different than ours. Compared to canines, humans don't have a sense of smell. When I ask a dog about the other dogs in the house, he will send me very detailed information in the form of scent, but I might vaguely smell 'dog.' Animals try very hard to communicate with us and once a dog realizes that I am severely handicapped, he will switch to mental images of his companions, which I understand.

Every animal has a unique energetic feeling to them. An example of this is when you know which of your three cats jumps on the bed, even though it is dark and you can't see them. A healthy four-year-old dog has a very different energetic feeling than a 15-year-old with cancer. The **Moving Energy Down and Up** exercise is an introduction to this concept and the following is another exercise to help you experience your own unique energy. **Feel Your Energy.** Clap your hands together and squeeze them tight. Pretend they are stuck and forcefully pull them apart about six inches. There is something between your hands. You can press on it, let it expand or set it down on the table. It might feel like a smooth ball, a fuzzy pillow or static electricity to you. If

Chapter Two: Awareness and Focus

you bring your hands close together and choose to not let them touch, they won't. Some people describe this like playing with magnets; your hands resist each other. This is your unique energetic signature. This is another way to check in with yourself. By becoming familiar with your own energy, the more sensitive you'll be to someone else's.

I usually start a reading by moving energy through an animal's body and noticing where I feel resistance. Healthy bodies have little resistance and the energy flows smoothly. Pain is a major energy disruption and noticing where energy *sticks* and doesn't move helps me determine if the animal has a disease or injury. Many times, I am drawn directly to the part of their body that is painful or weak. I often touch the weird little lump or the knee that had surgery when I first meet an animal. I have practiced this skill for many years but it is difficult to explain, as it is a very intuitive process. You may not be able to tell if a cat has kidney problems by touching his back, but you can develop your awareness to a level that can have a large impact on your animal's life.

Being able to identify the normal state of your animal's body will help you notice when something changes. A woman who attended one of my classes shared an example of why this is important. She was petting her dog and noticed a tight feeling in her own stomach. She didn't really think anything of it until it happened again and she noticed her dog was just not quite himself. She had the foresight to take him to the vet and they kept him overnight. About three in the morning, he started pacing, pawing at his belly and had violent dry heaves. They did emergency surgery and found several feet of dental floss wrapped around his intestines. Her ability to detect her dog's change from normal and her willingness to take action saved her dog's life. Another lesson, make sure your dog can't get into *any* trash. They can and will eat non-food items that can kill them.

This woman felt something in her body and was able to associate that with her dog. This is called a referred sensation. I use this type of information to help me identify dysfunction in an animal's body. If I am working with a horse and feel a sensation in my left shoulder, for example, I will focus on their left front leg. I don't feel the pain as if I was injured, it is more like when you walk by the stove and realize that you left the burner on because the air around it is warmer. In working with all kinds of animals, I have found that knowledge of anatomy is not terribly important when getting physical information from them. I don't need to know all the structures of a horse's foot to feel the pain and inflammation from overwork. Nor do I need to know the name of the vertebrae to tell where a dog's back hurts. I always tell an animal what I'm going to do before physically touching them. I tell them "No hurting, just touching," because many animals associate having a stranger touch them with going to the vet. I tell them exactly what I am going to do and do exactly what I said I would, giving them every opportunity to trust me. I don't say, "I am going to touch your ear" and then touch their tail. Some animals won't let me touch them and I never insist on it. I have lived with Monster for over a decade and have never petted her belly.

The most basic level of physical awareness is evaluating the information you receive when you touch your animal. You can train yourself to take your animal's relative temperature. Your fingertips are sensitive enough to tell about a 2° F (1° C) temperature change. Just to keep your human ego in check, a cat can detect a 1/10 ° F change on their pads. The next time you stroke your dog's ears, really feel the tempera-

Chapter Two: Awareness and Focus

ture with your fingers. Do this regularly and ask yourself, "Does this temperature feel the same as it did yesterday?" Or, "Is one ear warmer than the other?" It isn't important to know that a dog's average temperature is 101 to 102.5° F (38.3 to 39.2° C), but it is important to notice the change from one day to the next. If you have more than one dog, you need to feel what is normal for each one because one might have a higher base temperature than the other. You are trying to detect when something changes from normal. Ear infections are painful and dogs that have long or heavy ears are prone to them. The more you practice this, the sooner you will be able to detect a fever or an infection and the sooner you can get them treatment. Don't wait until your dog's ears stink before you take a look inside.

Understanding what is normal for your animal can help you detect changes in their health. Your left brain is excellent at comparing quality and quantity. Actually look at the size and number of clumps when you scoop your cat's box. A change might be your first clue that your cat has diabetes or kidney disease. When you run your hands down your dog's sides, do you notice that he no longer has ribs? Ribs are not hypothetical; you should be able to feel them. If you can't, you need to take action and make some changes in his diet and exercise. You can also choose to ignore this information and have your vet tell you your dog needs to lose twenty pounds because he is obese.

Pay attention if you feel a bump on their skin that wasn't there previously. Light colored animals or those with little hair can develop skin cancers, especially on their nose and ears and you need to check them every month. Carefully examine any lumps and notice if they have grown or changed. Take some pictures and compare them over a period of time. Some dogs (Labs in particular) get lumpy as they age. Often these are just cysts or fatty tumors, but they need to be evaluated. I have seen dogs with fatty tumors the size of footballs that were inoperable because the people waited too long to get treatment. Just like with people, taking action when you first notice a change leads to better outcomes.

An animal's physical condition has a direct impact on their behavior. Cats with urinary tract infections can associate their litter box with pain and refuse to use it. Dogs that have food intolerances can be hyperactive and hard to train. I worked with a dog that had been adopted and returned to the same rescue group three times. He was a sweet dog, but people complained that he just had too much energy and wouldn't settle down. I did a food evaluation on him and determine that he reacted to corn in his diet. Once they switched him to a new food, he calmed right down and learned basic obedience commands very quickly. This small change helped him get into a permanent home.

Conscious Touch

Be mindful of how you touch your animal. People often tell me, "I'll be petting my cat and she just bites me. I don't know why." The cat will be fine for a few strokes, and then give a swat or bite and jump off their lap. This is because the person is not paying attention to their physical interactions. Cats are very sensitive to touch and we are clumsy oafs, often petting them like dogs. If you know the cat bites if you touch her near the base of the tail, stop doing it. Consciously choose to stop petting her about three-quarters down her back. Maybe she has a sore muscle, a pinched nerve or maybe it just annoys her. Whatever the reason, when you keep touching that spot, you create a lot of needless stress

Chapter Two: Awareness and Focus

for everyone. No behavior exists in a vacuum; you are either making it worse or making it better. By engaging your observational and analytical brain when you touch your cat, she avoids a painful tweak in her back, you avoid a bite and you both have the opportunity to enjoy spending time together.

Animals don't always understand human intent and many misinterpret how we touch them. Patting an animal on the head can seem like hitting and can be a very stressful for an animal that has been abused. Hugging an animal around the neck can also be upsetting. Some animals get used to hugging, but many don't. Dogs often take this as a sign of aggression and it puts your face very close to theirs. This can result in very traumatic bites, especially with kids. Predators attack horses in the throat and they can panic when you throw your arms around them. Teach your kids not to hug animals they don't know.

Conversely, touch can be very reassuring to an animal when they are anxious or stressed. Stroking an animal's ears to the tip or rubbing their chest can help soothe them. Dogs and cats also have a place near the top of their head that, when you apply gentle pressure to it, helps calm them down. I call this the **Magic Spot** and it is a great way to make a physical connection with your animal. For both dogs and cats, there are two little ridges that start at their eyebrows and come to a "V" near the top of their head. When you put steady, *gentle* pressure on the narrow end of the "V" for about fifteen seconds, most animals will noticeably relax and some seem to melt as if they have no bones. The key is to use gentle pressure. If you push too hard, it gives the animal a headache and it will agitate them. Don't tap on the spot or increase the pressure; keep the pressure steady and consistent.

If you have a dog with a particularly round head, like some Chihuahuas or Boston Terriers, the **Magic Spot** can be tricky to locate, but if you are sensitive to the physical and energetic information from your fingertips, you will find it. If you look closely, many times there is a mark on the animal's coat over the spot. I have seen many examples of nearly solid color animals that will have a few white hairs right there. If you can't find the exact spot, put your whole hand on the top of their head and concentrate on feeling calm and relaxed. Send your energy into the ground, like in the **Moving Energy Down and Up** exercise. This technique is useful when you need to get some physical control without using force, like when someone is coming into the house or taking an animal to the vet.

Horses are a little different; their spot is more to the front because of the shape of their heads. Imagine an "X" from the inside of their ears to the inside of the opposite eyes. The spot covers more area on a horse's head than a cat's, so you may need to use your palm instead of your fingertip to apply pressure. Just because a horse is larger doesn't mean you need to press harder. Focus on feeling calm and relaxed while keeping the contact steady and gentle. You are not forcing anything. Instead, you are allowing less intense emotions to flow through you and your horse. I often use this technique when I first meet an animal as it helps keep them from becoming overly excited. This is a very calming technique and it can quickly de-escalate a reactive situation.

Another way to get physical control of a dog is to put light pressure on their muzzle. This is how a mother corrects her puppies and says, "Listen to me because I'm the mom and I need you to cooperate." This is a slightly dominant position to take with the dog, but not an aggressive one. Use a minimal amount of force to get the animal to work with you instead of against you. I will hook one or two fingers over the top of their muzzle and apply a little pressure to move their

Chapter Two: Awareness and Focus

head so they look at me. I like to make eye contact when I communicate with an animal. I am not trying to close their mouth or force them to do anything. I just want them to work in partnership with me. You have to adjust the amount of pressure to the size of the dog and obviously this doesn't work with dogs that have very short faces like Pugs or Shih Tzus.

Dominance Versus Affection

Put your observational skills to good use by noticing how your animal deliberately touches you. Confusing dominance with affection is one of the most common mistakes people make with their animals. When your dog sits in front of you and puts his paw on your lap, it does not mean "I love you," it means "I own you." When your cat head butts you, she is scent marking you and claiming you as property. When she weaves around your feet, she is not saying, "You're the best mom, ever!" She's saying, "Mine, mine, mine!" like the seagulls in the movie *Finding Nemo*. When an animal uses its body to influence your behavior, it is usually being dominant.

Often an animal is very good with one person and rude with someone else. The lenient person often refers to themselves as a "softy" or insists that the animal doesn't listen to them. This person usually has a part-time job letting the animal in and out or acting as a treat vending machine. If you can't sit down for five minutes without getting up to do your animal's bidding, your relationship is out of balance and the animal is manipulating you. This is not a partnership, as the animal calls all the shots. Pay attention to how the animal interacts with the other person and ask them to explain what they are doing. Just because a relationship has been unstable for a long time doesn't mean it can't change.

If you look at one action in isolation, it can be hard to determine if it is a show of dominance or affection. When a dog licks your face in an affectionate way, it is very fast and is accompanied with other happy body language, like a wagging tail. When a dog attempts to influence your behavior, she will lick your hand with a steady rhythm to get you to notice her. When the cat rubs against your leg and gives you a little tail hug, this is saying "Hi" when you have just walked in the door. But in another situation it can mean she is trying to get you to feed her for the fifth time that day. When your animal is intentionally touching you, use your critical left brain and look for other clues like: Is the animal looking at your face? Do they seem happy to interact with you or are they absolutely focused on the outcome? Are their eyes hard and intent or soft and gentle?

Animals are very good at getting what they want. If you have a large dog, you have probably experienced the dog leaning on you. When you sit on the couch and the dog is next to you, many times he will push against you. You move over. He pushes more. Pretty soon, he has taken over your spot and shoved you to the far side of the couch. Dominance is not necessarily a bad thing, but the animal is trying to control your behavior. Ask yourself, what is the animal's motivation in doing the action? Identify what is going on and decide what you are going to do. Will you repeat your long standing pattern or try something different? If you have just sat down and the dog puts his paw on you so you will get up and let him out, look away and physically remove his paw from your body, for example. Don't show any emotion, make it an automatic response. If your cat relentlessly head butts you to get you out of bed to feed her (two hours before her regular feeding time), blow in her face and put her off the bed. If it is a half hour after she usually eats, get up and feed her. When you are conscious of your physical interactions with your animals, you can respond in a thoughtful manner instead of just mindlessly reacting.

Mental Awareness

Mental awareness is an essential part of animal communication. How we think about and talk about relationships reflects how we feel about them. We are many times more intelligent than our domestic companions, but too often we disengage our brains and don't relate to our animals in a connected way. Things we overlook or accept without question often become emotionally charged problems. Relating to your animals when you are on autopilot creates mediocre relationships that are defined by negative emotions.

It is very easy to interact with animals without really engaging them. We absently pat them on the head, let them in and out and dump some kind of food in their bowl. Then we are shocked when they misbehave. So much of our behavior is automatic; humans have an exceptional ability to function in neutral. Because animals live in the present and are emotionally aware, they know when you are attentive and when you are not. Have you ever noticed how your dog will walk nicely by your side and then act like a barbarian when you check your phone? You have shifted your interest away from the dog and he will do whatever it takes to get it back.

If you choose to direct your energy to a single issue, you will be much more effective than when you are multi-tasking. When you focus on something, you give it meaning. Our companion animals desire to relate to us in emotionally relevant ways, but many have learned how to get large quantities of low quality attention. They will manipulate you in any way possible to get their needs met. When they don't get the type and amount of attention they need, animals can become obsessed with getting any kind of attention and their behavior becomes more extreme. If your cat continually walks across your keyboard, what do you do? Mindlessly put her on the floor. She gets some attention, but does not get your focus, which is what she really desires. If you tear your eyes away from the screen for a moment and consciously interact with your cat, or even get up and play with her for five minutes, it is highly likely you will have satisfied her need to relate with you for a moment and she will leave you alone to get something done.

Your dog is not sitting around worrying about how his stock portfolio is doing, so he has a lot of time and energy to devote to getting you to do what he wants. He experiments until he finds what makes you react; he learns how to push your buttons. The more his needs go unmet, the harder he pushes and the more automatically you respond. Around and around you go, each of you playing your part in the never-ending drama, generating more and more negative emotions. If you are not actively engaged with your animal you are creating your relationship by default and are giving them control of every interaction. Many people consider themselves to be their animal's parent. It is hard to be the parent when you operate on the same mental and emotional level as the baby.

When humans do direct our attention to just one thing, we focus on *Doing*. Animals are focused on *Being*. They live in the moment and use their energy to create positive experiences. Dogs are concerned with social status, where they are in the pack. Cats are obsessed with territory. They are very interested in their stuff and their space. Horses desire partnership, as they are herd animals. Working together with others is paramount for them. Will focusing on your animal

Chapter Two: Awareness and Focus

solve behavior problems? Not by itself, but it is an essential part of creating better relationships and is the first step in changing behavior. Could you really give each of your animals your complete, undivided attention for five minutes a day, every day? Can't hurt, might help.

Some animals have a surprising understanding of human psychology and are master manipulators. I did a reading for a dog who could have won an Oscar, he was such a brilliant actor. Rocco had been feral and begged for food at a convenience store. There wasn't much of a pattern as to who would give him something to eat or when, so he had developed several ways to approach new people. He first came up to me with a sweet face and tried to lick me. When that got no response, he wagged his tail and put a paw on my leg. Then, he backed off and barked at me and when that trick still did not produce any food, he lay down and started to whimper. Most dogs have one, maybe two, effective techniques to manipulate people. The Brown Eye Torture (where they stare at you with the biggest, saddest eyes, ever) works on many humans. Getting a random person to share a bite of hot dog with him was a matter of survival and Rocco used four unique strategies, each employing a different emotion. Most people responded to *friendliness*, which was a submissive behavior. Putting his paw on me was dominance, barking was a form of aggression and then he acted helpless. It was obvious that he understood human behavior and could use it to his advantage.

I find his progression from confident to vulnerable behavior instructive. This could be seen as an example of how dysfunctional relationships develop. No one starts a relationship with the intention of generating a lot of stress and negativity, but relationships can devolve in a downward spiral if you don't actively participate in them. If physical, mental and emotional needs are not met in a relationship, an animal (or person) will try a different strategy, often relying on increasingly more extreme behaviors to achieve their ends. Animals all want real, emotionally relevant connections with us. When we don't interact in meaningful ways, we create unsatisfying relationships. You are the brains of the operation, so use your best assets and think your way to a better partnership.

Words and Vocabulary

We talk to our animals all the time, but what are we really saying to them? Hopefully, it is positive and improves the relationship, but many times it isn't. Try the following **Day of Silence** experiment. On a day when you can be home, don't talk to your animals. Don't do this with anger or hostility, just be quiet. Do not verbalize anything to them. Don't say, "Do you want to go for a walk?" "Would you like a treat?" or "Let's go play ball." Don't greet them, ask them questions, or use their nicknames. However, you can still interact; smile, make eye contact, touch them, play. Just keep quiet when you do it. See if you can make it an hour without speaking to them. Really challenge yourself and see if you can go two hours.

You will notice two things. First, they understand you just fine, and second, the silence is absolutely deafening and it takes a lot of effort to *not* talk to your animal. We give our animals too much information verbally because that is how we think. To their credit, they are excellent listeners but animals don't think in words and they exist perfectly well without them. Not voicing every thought that pops into your head brings you more into the moment and helps you align with your animals on a different level. I find not talking to

Chapter Two: Awareness and Focus

animals verbally to be an excellent way of understanding their thinking. Do the **Right Brain Breathing** exercise either before or during this experiment.

People tell me all the time that their dog understands every word they say. The dog is very engaged and carefully listens for words that have emotional meaning for her, but she doesn't think in language. A dog, with her toddler mentality, may understand about 200 words and phrases. To put this in perspective, there is a vocabulary of 223 words in *The Cat in The Hat* by Dr. Seuss. I love *The Cat in The Hat* and had a client who named her cats Thing 1 and Thing 2, but it is not *Hamlet*. The average adult knows between 20,000 and 40,000 words. Your dog understands less than 1 percent of the words you use, so you need to be specific with what you say to her. Cats are even less verbally attuned and may only recognize a couple dozen words. The more you talk to your animals, the more useless information they have to filter out.

Our animal companions want to work with us, but we often make it incredibly difficult for them to understand how to do that. Too many people say things like, "Stop sniffing and come over here, now! Didn't you hear me? I said, get over here!" with hands on hips, in an annoyed and slightly aggressive voice. Saying their name in a threatening way is not a command. When you say a long, drawn out, "Don't ..." are you saying "Don't bark" or "Don't move"? Be specific with the words you use with your animal.

Listen to your words and how you say them. Many animals understand the rise in pitch when you verbally ask a question and people often ask questions when they should give commands. It isn't "Come?", it is "Come." Or even better, "Come!" You are not requesting his participation, you are telling him what you want him to do. Use your superior verbal skills to tell your animal exactly what you want. An area where I often cross-country ski allows dogs to be off-leash on certain days of the week. The trailhead is always very congested and I recently came upon a scene of utter chaos. Some people were getting started and they had two large dogs that were running around like maniacs. One of the people said in a really whiny and annoying voice, "Winston, stop that. You're being too rambunctious! Oh sorry. He didn't mean to knock you down. Winston, don't run! *Please* come here?!" It was really obvious who was in charge in that relationship. I was hoping she would just give the command, "Come!" with some authority and put Winston on a leash, but she was not awake enough to actually take charge of the situation.

Responding to their behavior by saying, "No, no! Bad dog!" gets you nothing. The even more ridiculous, "No, no! Bad cat!" gets you nothing, plus a subtle look of disdain. Without communicating a clear message, you forfeit the authority that your BFHB gives you. When your dog barks his head off, don't say, "Hey, quit that! Shush! It's just the neighbor!" Use the command "Stop barking!" instead. Isn't that what you want, for the dog to stop barking? Tell him *exactly* what you want him to do. Spouting off an endless stream of words hasn't worked very well for you in the past, so try something different. Two hundred words are not a lot, so use words that mean something.

Animals think in non-language. Occasionally when communicating with an animal, I will get a word or phrase, especially if it has been repeated many times and said with emotion. The most common word I get is "Stupid." Animals are not stupid just because they don't think like us. Words convey emotion. Monster hears the words "good," "cute," "silly" and "best" many times each day. What do you say to your animals? **Write a list of words** that your animal hears

Chapter Two: Awareness and Focus

the most frequently in your journal. How would you feel if someone said those things to you? Would you describe your human friends or family members in those terms? What you say to your animal and how you say it reflects your feelings about them and the relationship. When you say something like, "You stupid dog, all you do is cause trouble," you create just that, trouble for yourself, the dog and your partnership. I had a friend who referred to her cat as a turd. Guess what his issue was? Pooping outside of his box! Coincidence?

Too many people refer to their animal as 'psycho' or 'crazy'. To me, this indicates a damaged relationship, where the person is only looking at the negative aspects and believing their self–talk. The only behavior they notice matches the classification and the positive aspects of the relationship take a back seat. They react to the animal as if he really is crazy and create low-quality, unsatisfying interactions.

When you say negative things about your relationship or your partner, you put all of the emphasis on the problems instead of the solutions. If 98% of your partnership is great, don't obsess about the 2% that isn't. So many people justify bad behavior by labeling the offending party in negative terms. "He's ADD; she's finicky; he's just high strung; he's always like that" are excuses for the limiting parts of your relationship. This is usually followed by a statement about why the situation can't change, giving the person a way to avoid taking responsibility. Saying, "I can't exercise my (dangerously overweight) dog because he has leash aggression" does not help solve the problem. Saying, "My dog drives me crazy" keeps you stuck on the unpleasing aspects of the relationship instead of working towards longer term improvements.

I have a cat with serious neurological challenges, but Monster is not crazy. Most companion animals aren't, but I have worked with a few who I can only describe as mentally ill. Some of the most messed up animals I work with come from environments that include drug or alcohol abuse or serious human mental illness. One dog at a shelter was a truly unique case. They called him Fetch because that is all he did, over and over and over. He had no joy in the game and did it in a weird, robotic way. He didn't avoid eye contact and had no problem being touched, but he would only focus on the ball. Anyone could throw the ball and Fetch would bring it back without so much as perking up his ears or wagging his tail once. I got him to sit down and show me his life. All I saw was fetching. I asked him, *Show me your person*, and I couldn't get more than a vague shape, but did get a feeling of someone that was extremely obsessive/compulsive. If they started to play fetch, they were going to throw the ball 800 times. There was no praise, no joy, no emotion at all, just repetition. I have worked with dogs who were bored with the game and one client had a dog so obsessed with 'The Ball' that she had to keep it in a plastic bag in the freezer, but Fetch's total lack of enthusiasm shocked me. I can't say if the person's mental illness caused the dog's, but it had completely overshadowed Fetch's life.

Listen how you talk to other people about your relationship with your animal. People get caught up in the stories they tell themselves (and everyone else) about why their animal's behavior is the way it is. I spoke to a man who had a ten-week-old puppy that refused to eat. This poor guy was on his third trip to the store that week, buying a different brand of food each time. The pup was teething and unenthusiastic about crunchy dry food. Making matters worse, the wife was hand feeding him, so he received a huge amount of emotionally charged attention by not eating. They also had another dog that was a total Hoover, vacuuming up anything even

Chapter Two: Awareness and Focus

remotely edible. He would shove the baby away from the bowl at every opportunity.

This couple had to immediately shift out of their story about how the poor little puppy didn't like his food. They had already taken a couple steps down a very slippery slope and were about to create a lifetime of feeding drama, with the puppy expecting a lot of human interaction anytime food was offered. Some suggestions I gave him included moistening the dry puppy food with low sodium chicken broth (the regular stuff has way too much salt in it, even for people) or giving the puppy some cooked meat. I also strongly recommended having a regular feeding schedule where they offered the easy-to-chew food in a bowl (not by hand) and picked it up after fifteen minutes. Sometimes babies are just not hungry. They can be in a growth spurt and are busy growing bones and muscles, but their internal organs haven't caught up yet. When it was puppy feeding time, the older dog needed to be outside, in a crate or on a walk so the puppy had time to eat his food in peace without being bullied. Everything they were doing to correct the "problem" just created a larger one because they believed the story they told themselves. It takes deliberate effort to move from a limiting point of view. Paying attention to the words you use about your relationship can help you do that.

One way we define an animal is by their name. A name has energy and you will say it many, many times over the animal's life. Most mythical gods and goddesses were jerks, so if you call your dog Athena or Apollo, don't be surprised if they live up to that. I did a reading for a very outgoing Boxer named Zeus. Boxers tend to stand on their hind legs and swat at things with their front paws, hence their name. He hit the center of a large plate glass window and shattered it. His person wanted to know if someone had tried to break into the house. I asked him what he saw and he showed me another dog that looked just like him, standing by the window. It was his reflection. This is another example of a person having a deep connection with their animal. His person had a weird feeling that she should go home for lunch that day, which she usually didn't do. She came home to a broken window and couldn't find Zeus. He was under the bed and had gone into shock because of the blood loss. Again, trusting yourself enough to follow through with a little piece of intuitive information about your animal can have dramatic consequences.

People often ask why I didn't change Monster's name when I got her. Partly, I didn't want to make things more stressful for her (and myself) by trying to teach her a new name. *Monster* is not inherently negative, just like *Princess* or *Max* are not inherently positive. To me she is like Cookie Monster, eccentric and a little reactive, but essentially good-hearted. She is also Monster because she is an unrestrained biter with other people and I want them to be cautious around her. I took her to the vet (always traumatic for both of us) and they asked the animal's temperament on the intake form. I circled AGGRESSIVE and put two exclamation points by it. The vet said, "That's an unusual name" when he came in the room. I was terribly unsympathetic when Monster bit him after he reached in the carrier and grabbed her by the scruff of the neck. Her name is not Sweetie Cupcake for a reason!

Emotional Awareness

We think differently than our animals, but emotions unite us and help bridge the gap between our thinking abilities and theirs. Emotions are hard to put into words because we

Chapter Two: Awareness and Focus

process them through the non-verbal parts of our brains. We can feel things intensely but lack the vocabulary to describe our interior landscapes. Being able to feel individual emotions and clearly direct them is an essential part of communicating with animals and a skill you can master.

Human emotion is powerful and has a huge impact on our animals but many times, we are not aware of what we are sending them. I had a rough day at work and when I got home, sat down with a glass of red wine. I foolishly put the glass on a stack of magazines on my loveseat (just for a second, while I took off my cruel shoes). Monster jumped up to investigate and wine went everywhere; my clothes, my loveseat and the nice beige carpet. I had my head in my hands, rocking back and forth, saying, "Oh, no! Oh, no! I can't believe this!" None of this was directed at her, I was totally at fault, but this was a huge emotional reaction from me and Monster's eyes were the size of plates. Ever since that one event, when she smells red wine, she hides. Her brain tells her that particular smell is associated with Mom having an emotional meltdown. Animal thinking is situational; she can't tell when that drama took place only that it did. She never thinks about her aversion to red wine until that stimulus is in her environment and then she takes action. Because I checked out mentally, I caused a needless emotional scene that influences her behavior years later.

Identifying Specific Emotions

It is useful to think of emotions being ordered, with those that feel universally enjoyable, like love and joy, at the top and those that feel universally unpleasant, like grief and depression, at the bottom. The **Emotional Staircase** illustrates that idea. Picture in your mind coming into a house with a small landing and directly in front of you is a staircase that goes up and one that goes down. Emotionally, the landing is neither positive nor negative. It is a place where very little emotion is present. The farther you move from this Neutral Point, the more intensely the emotions are felt.

First, go down the stairs into increasingly negative emotions. This is the emotional basement; it is dark, cold and unpleasant. Read this list of words (descending from the Neutral Point) out loud and really *feel* the associated emotion, waiting three to five seconds after each one. It is not necessary to think about a situation where you felt the emotion; all you have to do is experience it.

NEUTRAL POINT

BOREDOM

FRUSRATION

WORRY

JEALOUSY

ANGER

DEPRESSION

GRIEF

FEAR

HATE

Notice how you feel as you descend into stronger negative emotions. Also notice how quickly you were able to move from a slightly negative emotion to an intensely negative one. It is pretty easy to fall down the stairs into increasingly negative emotions. It is important to go down first and then up so you don't finish this exercise in an uncomfort-

Chapter Two: Awareness and Focus

able mental state. Now read the list in reverse order, climbing back up to the Neutral Point. If any of these emotions were particularly difficult for you to experience, stop and do the **Automatic Writing** exercise to help process what you are feeling.

Now, shift your attention and move up into the positive emotions. This is like climbing into a tower. It takes effort to climb up, but at the top is a window with a beautiful view. Again start at the Neutral Point and read the words out loud, pausing a few seconds between each one to really feel the emotion.

JOY
    LOVE
        HAPPINESS
            ANTICIPATION
                ENTHUSIASM
                      CONTENTMENT
        NEUTRAL POINT

There is no need to go back down. Stay in the very positive emotions as long as you can. These are the feelings your animals want to share with you. Recognizing positive emotion when you experience it puts you and your optimistic animal on the same page and is an essential skill for building satisfying relationships.

The point of this exercise is to connect with the individual emotions and feel how you shift from one to another. Awareness is not the same as analysis. You need to feel the emotion and really experience it, but you don't have to categorize or relate it to anything else. If love is a higher emotion for you than joy, or depression feels worse than grief, reorder the steps.

It is easier to move within one type of emotion (either positive or negative) and it takes a considerable amount of effort to shift from negative to positive. Switching between negative and positive emotions is like crossing the landing on a real staircase, you have to turn around and face the opposite direction. You need to consciously change your outlook. Become sensitive to when you shift from feeling a positive emotion to experiencing a negative one. Practice moving back and forth between the slightly negative sensation of boredom to the slightly positive one of contentment until you can really *feel* the difference. How does each emotion feel in your body? Does your posture change? How do your thoughts differ when you feel bored or content? Were there any emotions that were particularly difficult for you to feel or those that overwhelmed you? Write these observations in your journal. Practice moving up and down the **Emotional Staircase** until you can clearly identify which emotion you are feeling at a particular time.

Depression is a very negative emotional state and one I have personal experience with. When you are depressed, people give you a lot of advice. One of the brilliant things they share with you is, "Just snap out of it. Think about something happy." Of course, if you could do that, you wouldn't be depressed. Better advice would be, "Pull your sorry butt out of bed and get angry." You can't jump up the staircase all the way to happiness from the very negative feeling of depression, but you can drag yourself up one step to anger. You have to work your way up, step by step. That's not to say that anger is a positive emotion, but it just may feel better to you than depression.

Chapter Two: Awareness and Focus

Some people are surprised that I have hate on this list. Most animals never go down that far into the emotional basement, but some do. I have met a few animals that hate people but they are extremely rare. Animals are strongly biased towards positive emotions and when you choose to experience your glass as being more than half full, you come more into emotional alignment with them. If you are happy or even just pretending to be happy, your animals will reflect that back to you.

In a small sense, positive emotion is exactly what your animal wants to communicate with you. Animals seek joy and expect to find it. They are strongly biased towards you, their person and they want to share their joy. By creating positive emotion and actively expanding it (climbing up the staircase), you can change your life. On a larger scale, positive emotion is the foundation for more profound feelings like trust, empathy and compassion. You can share those higher level emotions with *all* animals, people, even the planet itself. Developing your empathy helps you use your actions to generate good, in whatever form that takes.

Animals know a lot about compassion. I had food poisoning and was miserably ill. Monster, who is not a snuggly cat and does not sleep with me very often, was by my side the whole time. After I regained some sort of cognitive function, I found that she had tucked White Mousey in bed with me. White Mousey used to be a cloth mouse, but through constant licking, its whiskers, ears and tail have long since disappeared. She couldn't go to the store and get me some Gatorade, but she could show compassion when I needed it the most. She understood that White Mousey would help me because it helps her feel better when she is stressed. My heart filled with gratitude and I did feel better. I was truly touched by this act of caring from my strange cat. I use this as a benchmark for people in my life. Does their behavior show as much empathy as my cat did on that occasion? Too many people talk about compassion without showing it. Compassionate action matters.

Love is an incredibly powerful emotion. Saying, "I love you" to your animals is just so many words unless it is accompanied by the strong emotional bond that you feel for them. When said with authentic sentiment, the words "I Love You" make a contract. Your part of that agreement is you will care for the animal with compassion and respect for their entire life. The animal's part is that they will give back to you the love you give to them a hundred times over. They will not judge you, criticize you or say anything mean to you. They will love you unconditionally, even when you get caught up in Doing instead of Being.

This **Feeling and Focusing Love** exercise helps make the words "I Love You" much more significant. Animals strongly desire to feel this intense emotion from you and it is as important to their well-being as food and exercise. You can do this exercise face to face with your animal or with a photo. If you do this exercise with your animal, check in with yourself first and determine where you are physically, mentally and emotionally before you start. For example, I have a hard time communicating with animals when I am hungry because the whole conversation is about food. Control the physical environment so it is calm and completely dedicate your time to your animal. Look deeply in their eyes and just be in the moment with them. If you do this with a picture (like when you are traveling), have the picture ready before you start.

Chapter Two: Awareness and Focus

Close your eyes and imagine you are holding a beautiful bowl to the center of your chest. The bowl can be anything, crystal, gold, colorful ceramic or intricately carved wood; whatever is pleasing to you. Fill the bowl with every warm, fuzzy, positive emotion that you can. Whatever love feels like to you, put it in the bowl. Imagine these warm feelings as gold or green light and let them flow from your heart into the bowl. Feel the warmth in your body.

Open your eyes and allow the contents of the bowl to pour out onto the picture of your animal or directly into your animal through their eyes. Picture your animal surrounded by light. Know that they are receiving what you are sending them. Feel the animal absorb this energy and send it back to you. Accept this as a gift. Feel the animal's gratitude for this exchange of energy.

How do you feel when you make this connection? Check in with yourself and identify how you feel physically, mentally and emotionally. Imagine a beam of light joining you together. Notice when their pupils dilate. This is how you know you are communicating with them. You don't have to hold this connection very long, just deeply feel the love flowing between you. Allow the animal to walk away or go to sleep if they choose. Write about your experience in your journal or do the **Automatic Writing** exercise. Practice this exercise often.

Expressing these positive emotions reminds you of the strong attachment you have with your animal companions and is the foundation to creating better partnerships. Emotions are contagious and can easily be transmitted between people and animals. Thinking about what you love about your animal is a good way to move up the emotional staircase at any time. This is why you have a picture of your cat on your desk at work; you feel positive emotions when you look at her cute face and that helps you deal with other, not so pleasant feelings.

Thinking About Emotion

The previous list of emotions is pretty basic and these are the emotions animals most often share with me. Humans are able to express nuanced levels of emotion; there are many more steps on our staircase than a dog or cat's. Animal emotions are more direct and intense. They often mirror their human's emotion, but in a simpler way. If you are annoyed about a property line dispute with your neighbors, for example, your dog may act aggressively towards them. Animals don't feel emotions that have a mental component to them like equality, justice or self-doubt. Revenge seems to be a uniquely human concept; you try to change how you feel about an event from the past with an action in the future and obsess about it in the present. This is pretty convoluted thinking and it is not available to animals. They don't try to *get back at you*, but they are very good at using their bodies and their behaviors to express how they feel. A woman was convinced the cat was trying to kill her toddler by tripping her at the top of the stairs. The cat really didn't like the kid and wanted her to go away, but premeditated murder was beyond the cat's intellectual capacity.

This is where you and your animals differ; they feel emotions and react to them, but you can think about emotions and change them. This takes determination and effort, but your ability to change the emotion you are feeling is essential for building better partnerships. You don't have to let your emotions define your life. When you notice you are in a reactive, non-thinking pattern with your animal,

Chapter Two: Awareness and Focus

take a moment to determine what step of the **Emotional Staircase** are you on and where you want to go. Decide if you want to move up, down or stay on the same step. If you take the time to think before you respond in an emotional situation, you will be less likely to overreact. Let go of the story you tell yourself about why you feel a certain way. Become aware of the emotional signals you send out. Your animal is very aware of them. You will use contrasting emotions to effectively change your animal's behavior, so this is an important skill to practice.

Your internal dialog may go something like, "At this moment, I am feeling Emotion X. Is that an appropriate emotion? Can I choose a different emotion right now?" In order to move from an even slightly negative emotion (like worry) to a positive one (like anticipation), you need to take many intermediate steps, always moving to an emotion that feels better than the one you are experiencing at the moment. The emotion you are feeling affects how you react physically in a given situation. Are you really as furious as you are acting or are you just frustrated and don't know what to do next? Once you develop this type of acuity, you become less reactive and can use your left brain to create a better response when your animal pushes your emotional buttons. Emotions, when expressed in a controlled and deliberate manner, become a powerful tool to change your animal's behavior.

I read on the Internet (so it must be true) that if you yelled nonstop for eight years, you would expend the amount of energy needed to heat a cup of coffee. Probably more metaphor than fact, this still illustrates an important point; staying in a negative emotion is incredibly futile and destructive to all of your relationships. Deliberately, willfully and consciously choose a positive emotion any time you can. This simple act changes your attitude about the relationship in general, the words you use to describe it and how you relate to your partner. Positive emotions increase your resiliency so when things do go wrong, you can bounce back quickly instead of getting mired down in increasingly unpleasant feelings. Try this experiment: when you are **waiting at a stop light**, identify the emotion that you are feeling. You have many options available; you can feel bored, frustrated or furious; emotions ranging from slightly to very negative. You can also choose to be relaxed and happy, or even delighted to have a small break in your busy day. If you are in a meeting at work, you can select between being bored or being content. The emotion you pick will change how you experience an event. Could you choose to experience a positive emotion over a negative one once a day? Twice? Twenty times? How would that impact your life? Try it and find out.

It can be very challenging to feel anything positive about your dog after he jumped on the counter, got a box of brownie mix out of the cabinet and ate it in the living room while you were at your friend's birthday party. This happened to one of my clients about two weeks after she adopted a new dog. Imagine yourself in this situation. You could go off like an emotional volcano, spewing negativity everywhere or, you could acknowledge your shock and disappointment and *not* react in a way that would damage a very new relationship. Staying mad at the dog and replaying this tragedy again and again in your mind is one option. Recognizing how quickly he tries to make up to you after you corrected him is another. You can use your BFHB to manage your response in an emotional situation, but only if you know where you are on the **Emotional Staircase** to begin with. This woman is my

Chapter Two: Awareness and Focus

hero because she not only kept the dog but also enrolled in obedience classes. She wasn't even too upset about having to replace the rug.

An interesting thing about emotions is they don't have to happen in real time to be impactful. For both you and your animals, remembering an emotion is often just as powerful as experiencing it the first time. Think for a moment about being cut off in traffic. Really put yourself in that scene. Do you feel suddenly alert? Can you feel the rush of adrenalin? Does your heart rate go up? Your memory of this event triggers your physical response, even though you are not in the situation.

The physical sensations associated with anxiety and anticipation are very similar (heightened alertness, shallow breathing, sweaty palms...) but the emotions are very different. One feels negative and you try to avoid it and the other feels positive and is something you actively create for yourself. These emotions vary quite a bit in intensity. For example, you can feel slightly anxious about getting to your meeting on time, or experience intense anxiety about public speaking. You may experience mild anticipation when thinking about a nice dinner with friends or extreme anticipation like a kid on Christmas Eve. You can always choose between feeling bad about something or feeling good about the same set of sensations. When you feel anxious, try shifting into eager anticipation (an emotion animals understand very well). Identify with the emotion of anxiety and mentally shift it by saying, "I'm excited! I look forward to this!" Fake it till you make it.

Emotions span the divide between our logical brain and an animal's reactive one, but we get into trouble when we think an animal feels the same way about a situation that we do, especially when strong emotions are involved. It is essential to understand that your emotions are not your animal's. They can very much influence each other, but your animal is the main actor in their life and they have a right to their own feelings. I spoke to a man whose dog and mother had died within a month of each other. He wanted to know how his remaining dog was handling the grief. The dog had gotten over her grief very quickly and was actually enjoying not having to share any attention or food. I told the man this and he got very angry, insisting that the dog was still grieving because the dogs were so close. He was projecting his grief onto the dog and couldn't believe she didn't feel the same way he did.

Being unaware is like being asleep. Things happen and you react without employing any of your advanced thinking skills. Understanding how you really feel about a situation helps you avoid escalating a mildly negative emotion into a much more damaging one. The physical and mental aspects of relationships are easy to describe in words. The emotional part is much more difficult. Practice **Automatic Writing** to give this unexpressed energy a voice. The more you practice mindfulness in all of your relationships, the more in control you will be and the more enjoyable your experiences.

Chapter Three:
Using Some of Your Best Skills: Visualization, Creating Expectations and Enforcing Boundaries

At this point, you have increased your awareness of your actions, thoughts and feelings. Creating visualizations is the next step in changing your animal's behavior. When we activate our visual right brains and think in pictures, we are able to get our animals to cooperate with us. Pretend, imagine, daydream and picture in your mind's eye are ways to describe this creative, non-verbal process. Anytime we create something, we picture (or hear or feel) it in our minds first, then we bring it into the physical world. Making mental pictures helps us do mundane activities like choosing a box to put something in. Visualization also helps create more insightful experiences, like understanding someone else's reality.

We can visualize events from the past, things that we would like to create in the future or imagine things that don't exist at all. If I ask you to picture yourself standing by the sink in your kitchen, you will be able to easily place yourself into a very specific image. That mental picture might differ from the dream kitchen that you want to build some day. You can also create the idea in your mind of a purple cow jumping rope on a bridge. Animals think in pictures and emotions. Visualization is an effective way to communicate with them and can turn conflict into cooperation. Use this natural ability to be in a like mind with your animals and help them understand what you want. Some people tell me they can't visualize anything, but I think they don't recognize when they are using their right brains. Believe that you can do this and allow yourself to be surprised.

One of the keys to building supportive partnerships between animals and people is to use your empathy and visualization skills to see things through their eyes and relate to their experiences. This is how you can improve their lives and open yourself to the more consequential aspects of your relationship with them. Many human actions are terrifying to animals. Imagine you are a young kitten or puppy. Your eyes and ears barely function, you can't move around very well by yourself and you are completely dependent on your mother. Some huge creature, a hundred times your size, comes stomping towards you. There is a blinding light and crashing noises. The creature changes shape, grabs you, lifts you way up in the air and moves you towards its mouth. Sounds like a horror movie! More likely, you came home from work, switched on the light, put down your package and took off your coat. Then you picked up your adorable little friend to give her a kiss. Routine for us, but truly frightening for a young animal. Use your empathy and advanced mental skills to relate to what you are creating for your animals.

I believe exchanging information with animals is an intrinsic human trait that enhances our kindness and compassion. People often ask me about the mechanics of this, how we are able to share impressions across species. This is an interesting philosophical question and I don't have a good answer to it. I describe communicating with animals like using the microwave. I have had engineers explain to me how this mysterious machine functions, but I still don't understand it. Nevertheless, I am able to use it very efficiently. I don't know how my mental pictures and feelings are understood by an animal or how their life pictures and strong emotions come to me. Maybe it is a spiritual connection, shared brain chemistry, quantum mechanics or the power of love. I have learned to work with this rather than question it. The really amazing thing is, you also have the ability to send images and emotions to your animals and they will understand them.

Visualization

Visualizations are little mental movies with an emotional soundtrack where you are the writer, the director, the main actor and also the audience. Essentially, you are making movie previews to decide which one you want to experience. Visualization allows you to test drive different scenarios and prepare your reaction *before* getting into an emotionally charged situation with your animals. Your right brain can create contrasting mental movies and your analytical left brain can evaluate them to make a plan of action. Animals use their emotion to control your behavior. When you apply your superior thinking abilities you can easily out think your dog, cat or horse, regaining control in the relationship. By using your right and left brain in conjunction, you can avoid getting into reactive or mentally disconnected exchanges with them. You will be able to anticipate your animal's behavior and prepare your physical, mental and emotional response in advance so you are ready to act when the time comes. Visualization helps you get out of situations where you and your animal partner automatically trigger each other's behavior.

It is easy to describe a process visually. I can draw a little picture story using stick figures (because I can't draw anything else) to show how I make coffee in the morning. One action follows another and there is a beginning, middle and end to this process. I would also draw a happy face, denoting the emotion I feel when I drink my delicious coffee. This is a very simple story coupled with one clear emotion. This story has enough detail to be relevant, but it is not important to know where I buy my beans or what type of grinder I use. Remember the cow? It had a color and did an action in a particular place. It is not important to know how big the cow is or what bridge she is on. Simple is better when making visualizations. Remember, your animal can't think like you so you have to make the effort to think like them.

Your mental movie for your animal should:

- Tell a progressive story; have a beginning, a middle and an end.
- Tell one story at a time and focus on one type (positive or negative) of emotion.
- Tell the story as clearly as possible, but still be specific.
- Be really simple, you are dealing with a toddler brain.
- Show the animal's part AND your part of the story from their perspective.

Making a mental movie is harder than it sounds because you have to let your right brain be in charge for a while and slow down your thought process, thinking in clearly defined steps. If you try to use too many images or mix positive and negative emotions in the same mental movie, the animal will not get the message. You want to picture one simple story with one emotion. I did a reading with a wonderful German Shepherd named Radar. He had weak hips and naturally

Chapter Three: Using Some of Your Best Skills

sat with his feet turned out, like a puppy. I did a little visualization with him, picturing him sitting with his feet exactly square and his person admiring him. I gave him the command, "Sit" and he did it perfectly. He just needed some specific coaching on what that was supposed to look like. He was able to understand my visualization and then do exactly what I showed him.

Without the emotional component, visualization is just some nebulous fantasy, a little brain doodle for your own amusement. By putting emotion with your vision, you make it real and connect to what is possible. For example, if you wish to teach your dog to come when you call, visualize this story: You call her, she stops what she is doing, looks at you and walks directly to you. That is an excellent mental movie! It is has a beginning, middle and an end and shows a specific action. Now add the emotional soundtrack about how you feel when you picture her coming the first time you call. The emotional part of a visualization is very general, don't strive for subtlety. Go big with the emotions you express. Are you thrilled that your dog came when called? Pretend that you are and visualize yourself being elated! This is your movie and you totally get to over-act. Greet her like she has a $100 bill in her mouth and praise her exuberantly! She doesn't know you are faking it. The best part is, your brain doesn't know you are faking it either and it will generate more positive emotions about the relationship. When you act happy and animated, you often feel happy and your interactions with your animals will be more fun.

Crafting the emotional soundtrack involves checking in with yourself and connecting to the emotions you experience when picturing an animal behavior. You don't need to determine why those emotions are associated with any particular mental image; just really feel them. **Practice making**

mental movies by visualizing a slightly annoying animal behavior that you would like to change. It can be anything from the dog stealing food, the cat scratching the couch or your horse not standing still when you attempt to mount her. Think about the mental movie like this: "When I visualize my animal doing behavior X, I feel emotion Y. Determine which step of the **Emotional Staircase** you are on. Are you frustrated, worried or truly angry? Do you want to change that emotion to something that feels better or pretend like it doesn't exist? What is the next scene in the movie? Are you yelling at your dog and punishing him? Is he cringing and looking guilty? Are you smacking your horse with the lead rope or jerking on her bridle? Does your cat ignore you and continue scratching until she chooses to stop? Notice if your feelings become more intense the longer you view the scene. Write this out in your journal.

Now visualize the animal in the same situation, but not doing the annoying behavior. The dog looks at the plate but does not lunge for it, the cat walks past the couch and scratches something more appropriate or your horse stands perfectly still while you get on. Does the emotion associated with this image feel better to you? Do you respond differently? What next? Are you going to move on to something else or share your positive feelings by praising your animal's good behavior? Write this scene out as well. Which movie do you want to watch more often?

By comparing two possible outcomes, you can change out of your automatic patterns and make a plan of action. You are conducting a thought experiment in the form of **"if this, then that."** Your script follows the format: When my animal does action A, I will *choose* to feel emotion B and *choose* to respond with action C. If my animal does not do action A, I will respond with emotion D and action E. This type of think-

Chapter Three: Using Some of Your Best Skills

ing gives you the ability to respond to an emotional situation in a non-emotional way.

Use visualization to mentally practice your actions before engaging your animal physically. Giving a cat a pill can be a challenge. Picture in your mind calmly walking up to your cat while she is peacefully sleeping, smoothly popping a pill into the back of her mouth and gently holding her mouth closed with her head tilted back, caressing her throat. She swallows the pill and goes back to sleep. Add your soundtrack to this movie and let your cat feel how much you love her, how grateful you are that she quietly took her medicine and let her know that you expect her to feel better. Simple, right?

Contrast this movie with the much more common one that involves you dreading giving the cat medication and stealthily opening the bottle, hoping that she won't hear it. Of course she does, because you have already alerted her physically, mentally and emotionally that something unpleasant is about to happen. She immediately bolts to avoid the experience that you have already invested with so much negative energy. You move the king size bed and drag her out, kicking and screaming. You use your overwhelming physical strength to pin her to the bed and pry open her clenched jaws. You force one of the pills (that you have picked up off the floor because you spilled them all) down her throat while she glares at you. Three seconds later, she spits the slimy pill onto your bedspread, exerts her authority by giving you a nasty bite and dives back under the bed. Repeat daily, or if you're really lucky, multiple times each day.

"**If...then**" mental movies are investment opportunities. Do you want to invest your time and energy into the gentle first example or the drawn out trauma-drama of the second? The payoff for this investment is a healthy animal and a loving partnership in the first case or a cat that gets another bladder infection (because you couldn't complete the antibiotics) and a relationship that is dominated by resentment and a lack of trust in the second. You have an equal opportunity to create a positive or negative experience from the same situation, so choose the outcome you want to see before getting involved in an increasingly negative interaction.

Don't get caught up in your own negative story about how hard it is to give the cat a pill. Visualize a different scene, feel a different emotion and expect a different outcome. If the cat makes a beeline for the most inaccessible spot in the house when you take the bottle out of the cabinet, change your pattern. If the pill bottle is always by the couch, it is very easy to give the cat a pill when she is relaxed and sitting next to you. Mentally practice what you need to do to be successful. For example, visualize the pill in her throat, where it will be swallowed, not in her mouth, where it will be spit out. With dogs, there are a lot of teeth and tongue to get past before getting the pill where it needs to go, so plan your delivery from the side, near the back of their mouth. Coating the pill with butter helps it slide down easily. Mentally write your script, rehearse your part and then act out your movie in real life.

It is very important to remind yourself *why* you are doing something unpleasant, you want to help your animal feel better. Visualize them returning to health and participating with you in the activities that they enjoy. This is particularly useful with horses, because their injuries can take a long time to heal. Picture your animal with a shiny coat and healthy weight, with the broken bones, torn cartilage, or surgery incisions completely healed. Create a mental movie of you playing and working together again, adding in the emotional sound track of how much you love sharing your

Chapter Three: Using Some of Your Best Skills

life with them. Visualize what you want to see in the future; you want them to be happy and healthy.

A client's elderly cat needed an insulin shot twice a day and this had become a huge strain on their relationship. The woman said things like, "I hate doing this. It hurts me more than it hurts him" instead of focusing on the benefit for the cat. She had to get out of the mindset that this was a battle, so I walked her through a visualization of quietly giving the injection. Once she accepted giving the shot as an active part of managing the disease instead of something to dread, I worked on the cat. I sympathized with him and acknowledged how tired he was because he had no energy. I explained that the little poke his mommy gave him would help him feel better. His behavior changed dramatically. Instead of hiding and hissing, he would lay down on the bed, anticipating the shot. They had the same expectations (that the cat would feel better) and were able to work together, which made them both much happier. If you are dealing with a situation like this, **Automatic Writing** is a good way to sort through your emotions, so you can get around them and actually work on solving the problem.

Creating Expectations

When you come home tired from work, have not even thought about dinner and have nothing in the fridge, what are you going to do? Order a pizza, of course! This is an act of overwhelming stupidity for me. I eat dinner every day, so it is not a huge surprise that I am hungry after work. If I actually bring the idea of dinner into my tired brain, I can get something on my way home or I could plan ahead and buy some real food on my day off. Ordering pizza means that I am not using any of my left brain cognitive abilities and am basically in a walking coma.

We have this same kind of disconnect with our animals. If you have a dog that is aggressive with other dogs, why would you expect everything to be fine when you turn him loose at the dog park? If you have never trained your dog not to jump on people, why do you expect him to calmly greet your grandmother when she comes to visit? The truth is, you don't really expect these things at all and are creating your experience by default. You can identify the animal behaviors that annoy you, but have you ever defined what you want to see instead? Many people have never given any kind of thought to what behavior they *do* expect from their animal.

Expectations are intentions with a backbone. When I create an expectation, I am willing to take action and bring it into the world. Compare these two statements: "I *intend* to have a well-mannered dog" and "I *expect* my dog to come every time I call him." The first one begs the questions: When? How? Are you talking about the dog you have now or some yet-to-be-named, future dog? The second statement helps you create a plan. "I expect my dog to come every time I call him *and* we are going to enroll in an obedience class to learn how to make that happen." Intentions are warm and fuzzy and make the inside of my head a nicer place to be, but they never seem to escape out into the real world. By setting an expectation, I have given myself a job to do.

It is important to develop the expectation that you can communicate with animals. Just like you expect the sun to rise tomorrow, expect to share information with your animal companions and improve their behavior. If you are inconsistent in your behavior and unaware of what you think, say and feel, you create your relationship through non-participation and your animal's behavior will reflect that. Without

Chapter Three: Using Some of Your Best Skills

having a clear expectation of their behavior, you relate to them in a mindless, reactive way. Your dog might come to you when he feels like it, or he might continue to blow you off. He is the main actor in his life and chooses to ignore you because what he does is more important to him. Focus on the behavior you want to see.

General and consistent expectations for behavior are much easier to enforce than specific or conditional ones. It is asking a lot for a dog, with her limited reasoning abilities to discern that it is acceptable to get on the old couch in the den, but not the nice couch in the living room. Teaching your dog which couch to get on will be very difficult if it's okay for her to get on the good couch when everyone is watching movies, but it is not okay any other time. If you really want her to understand this concept, every time the dog gets on the old couch she receives lots of praise, and every time she gets on the good couch, you correct her. Every. Time. It would be easier for her if you had the expectation that she not get on the furniture at all.

Animals and people both have expectations about the partnership and the closer those ideas match up, the better chance you have of creating peaceful coexistence. Everyone has to be in agreement about what the house rules are. Use your BFHB and your language skills to actually talk with the humans in the house about what animal behavior is expected and come to some consensus. Don't think for a moment your dog or cat won't play one person against another or the kids against the adults. Animals need structure and consistency and if they don't have it, they can become obsessively manipulative. Having well defined expectations helps you make a plan and reduce stressful experiences.

When I worked at the food store, people often brought their dogs in with them. One day, a woman brought in an adorable ten-week-old Lab puppy. I got a small cat toy and threw it for him, picturing him chasing after it. He picked it up, brought it directly to me and then sat down. This was an absolutely perfect retrieve, far exceeding what I thought he would do. He smiled ear to ear when I praised him. Everything about this was a good experience; he did something he was innately good at, the toy was the right size for him, my expectation was clear and he got immediate positive feedback. No clicker, no treats, no threats or bribes; just a clear expectation well matched to his ability. It would be so easy to keep going in this direction rather than having to re-train retrieving because he was given conflicting information about what was expected. Expectations are useful only when they are realistic and in line with what the animal is capable of.

Animals can't guess what you want and neither can anyone else in your life, so you have to tell them, specifically. If you are checked out mentally or emotionally and are not observing your own behavior patterns, good luck changing someone else's. Tell your partners what you expect. Deliberately create the movie and soundtrack for the behavior you want to see. *Visualize one action before giving one clear command. State exactly what you want and then expect your animal to do it.*

Expectations can also lead to problems. Imposing false expectations on your animal companions usually leads to behavior or health issues. Food creates many false expectations for humans and we transfer those to our animals. In too many cases, humans equate food with love. I had a client who made a *smiley face from canned whip cream* on a plate for her dog to lick off (everyday!). To her, this was love. She was in complete denial about her contribution to her dog's critical health problems and said the dog *needed* dessert. I see a lot of people who mistakenly expect their animal to enjoy the same things they do. I hate to break it to you, but your dog probably isn't thrilled when you dress him up and push him around in a stroller. A few find it fun, some put up with it because it gives you pleasure, but the vast majority really dislike it. Your dog doesn't know how to be a child, but he really enjoys being a dog and doing dog stuff.

Sometimes the difference between human and animal expectations is much greater. Jazzy had been at a sanctuary for four years before being adopted. She showed me pictures of her life there; she had a routine, lots of dog friends and she received plenty of attention from the staff and guests. Different people spent time with her everyday. The ultimate goal of all rescues is to get an animal into a forever home, but Jazzy was bored to death living by herself and she had never needed to develop a connection to just one person. She was also very frustrated at having restrictions on her behavior. She wanted to go back to the sanctuary. I explained this to the woman and she was crushed. She expected Jazzy to be thrilled at being an only dog and having a home. She had to let go of her false expectations and really focus on the day-to-day work of relationship building. It took about a year, but the next time I visited with Jazzy she was happy with her life. Expectations help get you and your animal on the same page.

Establishing Boundaries

So far, we have discussed the mindset of communicating with animals; you have to think like them in order to get your message to them. You have increased your awareness of the physical, mental and emotional aspects of the relationship and have become reacquainted with thinking visually. All of this is important, but it has pretty much taken place inside your head. How do you take these ideas and really change your animal's behavior?

People don't call me when their animal is a well-adjusted family member, they call me when the animal's behavior seriously impacts their lives. Many people have never put any boundaries on their animals and end up in destructive, negative patterns. Harness the power of your BFHB by defining what behavior is allowed and what isn't. You will enforce these limits with positive and negative emotions rather than force, thus bringing all of the mental preparation into the physical world. None of this is magic or *woo-woo* stuff (add your own air quotes if you like), just a different way of using your brain.

Because of our analytical abilities, we have authority in our relationships with animals. Authority means *the right or power to enforce rules; the power to act on behalf of somebody else.* Authority is based on trust and respect. Animals see you as being in charge, you create their world. It is essential that you accept this and lay down some rules about expected behavior. If you don't, you will live in a circus. Chances are, you can make better choices than your dog or cat. That isn't saying you will (especially if you have turned off your brain), just that you can.

If you feel like you have lost your authority in a relationship, do some small things to regain the feeling of having some control. Deliberately change your thinking and the words you use to describe your partner. Choose to take a different action. Have the courage to truly feel an emotion and select another one that feels better to you. Start small, act with conviction and celebrate your progress. Forget to judge, criticize or limit your experience and allow yourself to create more meaningful interactions. Help your partner work with you instead of against you. I am not saying you need to micromanage your animals, but have some idea of what you want to see. A man told me he had to tell his horse how to move each foot. I laughed out loud. We are pretty smart, but we know nothing about being an 1,800 pound quadruped. Horses know more about being horses than we do. Your relationship with your animal is a partnership, not a dictatorship.

Unacceptable is one of my favorite words. When you say it out loud, you draw a boundary, a line in the sand. Also, it sounds really important when you accent every syllable. UN-AC-CEPT-A-BLE! stands out from the endless stream of babble your animal hears every day. On one side, your animal's behavior *is* acceptable. It may not be perfect, but it is tolerable, appropriate and good enough. Cross the line and the behavior is no longer okay and you will take action to give a meaningful correction. There are negative consequences for crossing a boundary and positive consequences for choosing to not cross it. Your job is to clearly define where that boundary is.

When I help an animal change a behavior, I express approval and disapproval. I don't think in terms of dominance and submission or reward and punishment. I have the expectation that my cat, whom I feed, shelter, scoop her litter box and lavish with praise and affection will behave like a domestic companion animal, not a wild beast. Biting is unacceptable and I strictly enforce boundaries around this behavior. Monster bites at unpredictable moments, often without warning or a discernable cause. She has bitten me while I sleep, come into the house, leave the house, when I turn a page in a book and many other times as well. It hurts and I have scars from some of these attacks. This was almost a deal breaker in our relationship and is the largest generator of negative emotion between us.

If she bites, there is a predictable response to her action; I never just let it slide. I show her exactly what my emotions are: pain, anger and indignation about how rude she is. I stomp. I wave my arms and yell a lot. I am pretty sure my neighbors think I am emotionally unstable. Monster may be weird, but she is not stupid, so she runs and hides. I move furniture if she hides behind it. I get her cornered and I pin her to the ground, all the while saying something like, "That is totally UN-AC-CEPT-A-BLE! I will not tolerate you biting me! That really hurt and I am bleeding all over the place! *You will not bite me!*" Then I get right in her face and blow like I am blowing out birthday candles. This is a very intense interaction, but it only lasts a few seconds. When it is over, we both walk away.

Monster really dislikes it when I blow in her face and will use the tools at her disposal, avoidance and fighting, to resist this correction. She is fully loaded with claws and significant teeth. She will rabbit-kick the flesh off my arms and puts a lot of effort into trying to scratch my face during this interaction. It doesn't matter why she bit or how long it has been since the previous incident; if she bites, I pin her to the ground and blow in her face. This is carved in stone. I could just treat my wound and not correct her, thus avoiding more pain. That would be easier than confronting her but it wouldn't change anything. Because of always enforcing this boundary (and blood that clots quickly), Monster and I are able to live together in relative harmony. She has learned that biting is UN-AC-CEPT-A-BLE. From getting attacked several times a day, her biting me is now a rare occurrence.

I only use this correction for biting, nothing else. I had to mentally rehearse this when I was away from her so I could show strong emotion in a controlled way and I practiced with a stuffed animal to get the timing right. Even though

Chapter Three: Using Some of Your Best Skills

I have just received a painful cat bite, I have done enough mental preparation that I can concentrate on correcting the behavior instead of reacting involuntarily. I encourage you to express negative emotion, but think before you do so. You owe it to your animals (and yourself) to use force in a restrained and conscientious way. Using violence in response to Monster's behavior also makes the statement that her violence towards me is acceptable, which it is not. Becoming overwhelmed by negative emotions and punishing my brain-damaged cat would seriously diminish my humanity. Restraining her, like when I blow in her face, is using the minimal amount of force and is much different than hitting her. When I give her the UN-AC-CEPT-A-BLE rant, it is about how *I* feel about *her* behavior, not about her as an individual. It is not about belittling her or calling her names. I have the self-control to give her intensely negative emotional feedback in a non-violent way. You also have the self-control to do this with your animals. If you don't, you really need to look at why. Your relationship with your animals is an excellent mirror for other relationships in your life, past, present and future.

You decide where the boundary is and what will occur if the boundary is violated. Be consistent. Monster knows I will never hurt her, but I will show my displeasure in a way she understands if she chooses to bite me. I'm not shouting, "No, no! Bad Monster!" because that is just meaningless noise and it sounds really stupid when I say it. I use very focused emotions and specific actions to let her know her behavior crossed the line. None of this is subtle. I am not asking her to interpret anything. Blowing in her face is an effective correction because it comes directly from me, is immediate and is accompanied by a lot of negative emotion.

What is your intent when you correct an animal's behavior? To hurt and punish or enforce the boundary? What do you expect to gain from your action? Carefully controlled emotion is a very effective training tool when used in a way that will not harm the relationship. Simply reacting to your animal's behavior often means using too much force. This erodes the trust and respect that are essential to any partnership and creates more conflict. Set higher expectations for your behavior as well as your animal's. You have to decide what degree of naughtiness you will allow before getting caught up in an emotional situation. I have chosen which battles to fight and I ignore some of Monster's more eccentric behavior. I don't really care if she swats or hisses at me, but I do care when her teeth touch my skin.

When correcting a behavior, you need to align the emotions you are expressing with your actions. A client was very frustrated with her Pug, Gizmo. He would go into her office, knock over the trash, rip up the papers and then go to sleep in the trash can. She had very mixed emotions about this because it was naughty and made a mess, but it was also really cute. Because she found it appealing, it was very hard for her to correct the behavior. I had her visualize dealing with one emotion at a time. When she went into her office and found the dog asleep, she could take pictures and post them all over social media if she wanted. Then she needed to close the door and laugh her head off. When she was done, she opened the door and gave him a bunch of negative emotion about how unacceptable it was to get in the trash. She couldn't give an effective correction and enforce the boundary until her emotions and actions were congruent. This is why it is important to check in with yourself physically, mentally and emotionally *before* engaging your animal.

Chapter Three: Using Some of Your Best Skills

More than half of the people I work with let their dogs sleep on the bed with them. This is good place to draw a boundary. It is your house, your bed and you go to work to pay for it. Humans deserve their own space in their homes. You don't sleep in the dog's crate, that's his space and the bed should be yours. Coming on to the bed to snuggle can be a rewarding experience for both people and animals but it is by invitation only and the human decides when. The dog can sleep next to the bed. When the dog is on the bed, he shares your den with you, and basically doesn't have to do anything you say because you have the same amount of authority. If you have problems sleeping, having animals in your bed won't help. This is a very important boundary to draw as it directly impacts your health.

People make a mistake when they treat their dogs equally. Dogs are all about social hierarchy, they aren't equal and they can't even conceive of the concept. You can create boundaries to emphasize differences in status. If you have an older dog and get a younger one that is a relentless pest, help enforce the older dog's position. The older dog gets everything first; he is acknowledged first, let out first, fed first, in the car first. The younger dog is expected to "Wait" (given as a command, not a suggestion) quietly for his turn. Use your brain and decide where the boundaries are for each dog. What is a right for the older dog can often be seen as a privilege the younger dog has to earn. If the older dog is allowed off leash because he always comes when you call, that is a goal for the younger dog. Until he comes reliably, he will be on a leash. Dogs do understand fairness, however. It is fair that the young dog gets to go to the park more often and the older dog gets to go with you when you run errands. If they have different levels of physical endurance, walk them separately. They don't have to do everything in the same way.

Two Big Dogs

Your boundaries with your animals will be different than someone else's. Recently, I worked with two dogs from different families. Both were large, energetic, and about nine to ten months old. That seems to be the age when dogs just lose their minds. They are making the shift into adulthood and their physical need for exercise far exceeds their ability to work with humans. Kiwi was a very high energy Lab and was destructive. She liked to drag large branches into the house through the doggie door and then rip them apart in the living room and she also tore up shoes and books. She was smart and eager to learn, but her people never set any boundaries with her. She didn't pay any attention when they gave her a command because she had too much energy to actually think about what they wanted her to do.

I could tell they really loved her, but both the husband and wife worked long and irregular hours and they weren't giving Kiwi what she needed. I don't sugar coat anything with my clients and I told them what it would take to get her through the terrible teenage period: doggie day care two or three days a week, serious obedience training and at least a half hour of vigorous exercise every day. She would be a great dog in six months to a year. I asked them if this was the right dog for their family and I got a less than enthusiastic response.

They tried for a couple weeks to give her more exercise, but then she ate the couch. The woman called me in tears, asking what she should do. I advised her that she needed to re-home Kiwi. I try very hard to keep an animal in their home, but this situation was likely to end with the dog living in a pen or being taken to a shelter. This was a very hard decision for them to make, but it was the right one. It took

Chapter Three: Using Some of Your Best Skills

a couple of weeks, but Kiwi went to a great family who were looking for an energetic playmate for their dog. The woman later e-mailed me and said that she felt like a huge weight had been taken off her shoulders.

I had a case a few weeks later of another big dog, a Mastiff mix who was completely out of control. His person looked like she had been beaten up; she had so many bruises on her arms from him jumping on her and play biting with too much force. Jackson wasn't aggressive, just enthusiastic and about the same size as the woman. He would just go crazy in the morning, running around like a maniac, doing laps around her dining room table and she dreaded hearing the alarm. She kept him in a crate while she was gone, but didn't have a fenced yard. They were doing obedience training and he was clever enough to figure out that he only needed to mind when he was in class. She used to take him to a nearby dog park, but stopped because he frightened smaller dogs, so he had no outlet for his energy. I worked with the dog on the unacceptable behavior (jumping and biting) and showed the woman how to get him under physical control. I strongly suggested she find a way to finish fencing the back yard and I showed her how to use visualization with positive and negative emotions to get the behavior that she expected. When I left, this woman was very relieved and empowered because she could take back her authority in the relationship.

I can't consider the first example a failure because the result was the best thing for Kiwi. The second example was more of a success. The difference in outcomes was the willingness of the people to set and enforce boundaries. Jackson's person realized what she was getting into and had crate trained him at an early age. She also brought her expectations into physical form and had enrolled in obedience training. It wasn't terribly effective because he still had way too much energy, but the important thing was that she took action. Kiwi's people were not really prepared for what it meant to have an athletic dog and didn't try to set some limits until it was too late. For them to give the dog everything she needed would have meant a major lifestyle change. Even though it was a difficult choice to make, they did the right thing and found a situation where her needs would be better met.

Pushback

Maybe you have used your increased awareness of your dog's physical body to determine she needs to lose weight. You have made a plan and decided to count out the treats you will give her each day. Great! You are on the right track. How are you going to deal with the whining and near-constant begging that will follow? Are you ready to give your dog more play time or go on several short walks each day to distract her? Do you have a Plan B like feeding her a lower calorie food to help achieve your goal of improving her health? Think about a time you were on a diet. Was it a joyful experience you look forward to repeating? Probably not. When you suddenly can't have something, even if it was not beneficial, you become acutely aware of its absence. You focus on it incessantly and try very hard to get it back in your life. Animals (and people) will resist change with a vengeance. This is where expectations crumble into a pile of useless intentions. Be prepared for emotional pushback when you start enforcing boundaries within your relationships.

Animals like patterns and when you change them, they direct all of their actions towards getting you to revert back to what is familiar. Improvement is always possible, but

Chapter Three: Using Some of Your Best Skills

it won't happen overnight. Letting go of old, established patterns is hard for everyone. The more committed you are to changing your animal's behavior (by changing your own), the better you will be at dealing with the inevitable resistance.

Start with a small change that you can stick with. If you try to change everything all at once, you will lose your resolve very quickly when faced with even more bad behavior. Create realistic expectations and review your **"if...then" mental movies** frequently, always choosing the scenario that produces the most positive emotions. The important thing to remember is if your partner pushes back 20 times, be prepared to resist 21; don't get caught up in their drama. If you fall back to the old pattern, you are even further from your goal. Being inconsistent with treats, like when you are really good about limiting treats for a few days, then miss your evening walk and give more treats to compensate, creates huge problems. You are making that particular behavior even harder to change because your dog knows you will cave in. You don't have the backbone to stick with your decisions and if the dog acts in a certain way, she will get what she wants. Animals are very good at detecting our patterns and noticing our emotional disengagement, so use that amazing brain of yours to make a plan that you can live with. Pick your battles carefully.

Chapter Four: Changing Behavior

As you begin to change your animal's behavior, it is important not to try and change who they are. Your anxious dog is not going to suddenly become calm and relaxed. I taught Monster not to bite, for example, but I can't change the fact that she gets over stimulated because her brain doesn't work normally. Trying to change your partner is a waste of time. Devote your energy to changing what you can, your expectations, your emotions and your actions. Because animals naturally seek positive experiences and want to work in partnership with you, it is easier to change your relationship with them than any other in your life. Your animal's behavior will not change just because you want it to. Their behavior changes because you are giving them information in a different way and they understand what you want. When you notice improvements in your animal's behavior and the relationship produces fewer negative emotions, be confident that you are making the change happen. They are not just doing this to please you. Animals want their people to be happy but they also want to meet their own needs. Conflicts arise when their agenda and yours don't line up. Changing behavior through mindfulness takes time. It is much faster to use threats and bribes, but why would you want one of the most important relationships in your life to be based on a lack of trust or superficial interactions? Patience and persistence are two of our best human qualities, so use them to your advantage.

Chapter Four: Changing Behavior

Let's review the **mental preparation** needed to make a constructive change in your animal's behavior. You have to be mentally prepared to give a meaningful correction at the right time. If you are not, you run the risk of being overwhelmed with the emotion of the situation and reacting in an uncontrolled way. Take some time to really work through this exercise, focusing on one specific behavior at a time. Think about the benefits that will incur for you and your animal by making this change. Writing out your process step by step in your journal will be very helpful. There are no right or wrong answers, you are just recording your observations so you can review them later, making adjustments and refining your technique. Once you begin to see the behavior you expect, review your progress and celebrate your achievements. You can start with the behavior that occurs most frequently, causes the most negative emotion or that you feel is the most damaging to your partnership.

- Start with the **Breathing Exercise** and get into your right brain (block your right nostril). Visualize in your mind what happens to start the behavior, how it progresses and how it resolves (beginning, middle and end). Watch this scene from your perspective and again from the animal's. Make the movie clear and short. Stay focused on one behavior and edit out any extraneous information. Don't get off on a tangent.

- Analyze the emotions you feel when you watch this movie. Be specific and clearly define which emotional step you are on. Write your answers to these questions: How do your emotions change as you watch this movie? Can you define the point when you shift from positive to negative emotion or the negative emotion escalates? Does the emotion you feel stay with you after the movie ends?

- Try to understand the animal's emotion as they do the behavior. What do they get out of it? How do you appear to them? Is your behavior predictable and your response deliberate or are you a big over-reactive ape?

- Write down the words you use to describe the action and your emotional response to it. Are those words reflective of the relationship as a whole or just the emotional reaction to that specific behavior?

- Use **Automatic Writing** to clarify the emotions associated with this specific behavior. Write in the form: "**When my animal does X, I feel emotion Y.**" If this exercise brings up a lot of emotion about broader subjects, process those in a separate session. Stay dedicated to addressing one issue instead of shifting your attention or trying to change everything at once. The more you drill down on your emotions, the better you will understand your contribution to the behavior. These unexpressed emotions are obstacles to your progress, so giving them an outlet will help you move forward.

- Now use the **"if this, then that"** format (if my animal does action A, then I will feel emotion B and respond with action C. If my animal *does not* do action A, I will respond with emotion D and action E) to make another mental movie of the behavior you expect to see. Visualize your dog politely greeting someone or coming directly to you when you call him, for example. Again, tell one story with a beginning, a middle and an end, keeping it short and simple. Are the emotions associated with this mental movie different from those you experienced when you watched the first one? Write about this and notice the words you use to describe this scenario. Which visualization generates more positive emotion for you?

- Use the **Breathing Exercise** to shift into your left brain (block your left nostril) to really examine the two contrasting movies, especially your part in them. Use **"if this, then that"** thinking to make a plan of action. How will you respond differently? You are rewriting the script and directing the action. You are also one of the main actors in this mental movie and will play this part in real life. Repeat any of the above steps to analyze this new movie. Write out your script and refine it as needed.

- When the situation with this specific behavior arises, you will have done all of the preparation needed to act out this new script. Do you feel more in control of the situation? Does this exercise change how you feel about your relationship? Record your observations in your journal. Expect improvement and acknowledge it when you see it.

- Build on your success. Continue moving in a positive direction rather than getting frustrated and starting over. Give yourself credit for thinking your way out of a conflict.

This is the thought process that you will go through as you start changing your animal's behavior. Keeping notes of your process will help you refine it. I don't do this much mental preparation every time I communicate with an animal. This would be like relearning the alphabet before reading my email. This is a very condensed description of techniques I had to learn by trial and error. After you have worked through this process a few times and understand it, you will progress quickly. Like anything worth doing, animal communication takes practice. I use all of these techniques at different times, but the most immediate way to establish communication with an animal is to access my right brain through the **Breathing Exercise**. All of the practice falls away and I am in the moment, not *Doing*, just *Being*. After about three or four Right Brain activating breaths, I become receptive to their thoughts and feelings and am able turn off the chatter from my BFHB. In a way, you have to do all of the extensive preparation so you can then forget about it. Find the method that works best for you.

Approval and Disapproval

There are many options in every relationship. You can always choose to accept a behavior and not try to change it. If you won't change your own behavior, stop repeating your story about how terrible your partner's behavior is. Jessie Jackson said, "Both tears and sweat are salty, but they render a different result. Tears will get you sympathy, sweat will get you change." Take decisive action to move out of the problem and into the solution. If I think about how I don't like Monster biting me, I am putting all of my attention on the biting and the negative emotions it produces. I am focused on what I don't want. I can also envision her sitting quietly on my lap, purring while I pet her. I like that movie better; it has a much happier ending. Changing behavior takes a real commitment and a realistic perspective. Don't just go through the motions with your animals

Your goal should be cooperation rather than control. Get your animal to work with you by using approval and disapproval to emphasize a clearly defined behavioral boundary. Show your animal the emotional consequences of their actions. Make two visualizations: the *Naughty* movie (the behavior they are doing that you don't like) and the *Nice* movie (what you want to see). Visualize yourself expressing the negative emotions you feel about the behavior and using the UN-AC-CEPT-A-BLE speech. Don't be afraid to express strong emotion, just do it in a non-physical way. When you visualize the *Nice* movie, you show your animal how to please you. The soundtrack includes love, satisfaction and cooperation. Visualize yourself praising your animal when they do the right thing and really feel sharing that positive emotion with them. This is a controlled experiment, so you can focus on it intently and replay these mental movies when you are with your animal and away from them.

You are giving the animal an opportunity to create positive emotions in exchange for not creating negative ones. When you give praise, you are effectively telling them, "Yes! That behavior is strengthening our partnership. We are on the same path! Please do that again!" When you give a correction using negative emotion, you communicate, "We are not working together. We have conflicting agendas." This is different than saying, "Do it my way," by bullying or using physical force. Your goal should not be to win, or prove that you are the pack leader. It is essential to act out your part of the movie, just how you rehearsed it. If your dog sits when you tell her, but you don't praise her like you pictured in your movie, this process will not be effective. You need to follow through.

Use your large vocabulary to make praise meaningful. I have never found saying, "Good boy" to be very effective praise. Your dog is not a boy and he is not concerned about the duality between goodness and badness. Have you ever praised your cat? Most people never do. People will often pat their horse's neck after he has done something well. This doesn't convey any information. Your job is to tell your animal *exactly* how he pleased you. Pretend you gave a presentation at work. Afterwards, your boss comes up and says, "Good job." Are you a bit underwhelmed? Does it feel like she is only saying this because she read some lifeless management directive entitled *Motivating Employees*? Contrast this with your boss saying, "You did a great job on that presentation! I really appreciate how clear and concise you were when reviewing the data." Does this feel like she actually paid attention and was invested in the outcome? Which example would make you want to work harder?

Keep the *Naughty* and *Nice* movies distinct. If you combine the positive and negative emotion in the same visualization, your animal will get confused and not understand what you want. Keep the visualization the same and adjust the sound track as needed. It might start out with gentle disapproval in the *Naughty* movie and become more intense if the behavior gets worse, for example. Stack the deck in your favor and apply a disproportionate amount of positive emotion to the *Nice* movie. If you would be pleased when your dog sits on command, don't show him that. Climb up the emotional staircase and demonstrate that you are over the moon with joy that he sat when you told him to. Clap your hands and dance around! Throw a party for him! Let

Chapter Four: Changing Behavior

him know that this is the best thing you have ever experienced in your entire life. Your dog will be very eager to repeat the action that produced this crazy exuberance. Animals move toward positive emotion. The whole point is to get the animal to want to work with you.

I never use food when I work with an animal. Using food is easy, but bribes are the lowest common denominator of our relationships and make everything conditional. Your dog, cat or horse is smart enough to figure out they don't have to do something unless you give them a treat. Surely your highly developed brain can come up with something more sophisticated than enticing a dog to sit with a piece of cheese. Using emotional approval and disapproval can change your relationship from bad performance art into a respectful partnership. Let your animal know when they have done the right thing. Praise creates positive emotion for both the recipient and the giver. Make an effort to notice good behavior from your animal and praise them energetically. I realize it can be very difficult to muster any kind of enthusiasm at two o'clock in the morning when you take your new puppy out in the rain to go potty. Fake it, pretend, imagine or do any other mental trick that creates positive emotion and share it with your animal companion.

When I teach an animal a new behavior or change an existing one, I give them as much information as possible about what I expect. I use words, visual imagery, contrasting emotions (positive and negative), facial expressions and examples. In order to avoid a lot of standing around with the door open, I taught Monster how to ring a bell when she wanted to go outside. I had to break the process down into small, clear steps. I visualized her walking to the door (from her eye level) and reaching up to touch the bell with her paw.

I imagined the sound of the bell and what it would feel like for her to touch it. I added the visualization of me stopping what I was doing when I heard the bell, going to the door and opening it for her. I also showed myself praising her for being so smart and let her feel the self-determination of deciding when to go out.

A couple of times when she was near the door, I would gently take her paw (if she was willing) and touch the bell with it. Then I visualized the consequence of her action; the door opening and her getting to go outside. I replayed this movie over and over, the same process, the same details and the same positive emotions. Any time she was near the door I actively praised her. Keep in mind that Monster is not quite normal. She learned how to ring the bell to go out in three days.

At first, she was a little afraid of the bell and would touch it very gently. Then one day, she gave it a good swat. I enthusiastically praised her and opened the door. Before I could even close it, she was chasing another cat across the yard. I had just given her a wonderful new tool and she used it for her own purpose. Six years of college and I was outsmarted by an animal with a brain slightly larger than a golf ball. She reminded me that I am still the decision maker and I have a responsibility to actually check what is out there *before* I open the door.

When I have a discussion with an animal to change a behavior, I let them feel that their person loves them and that I am there to help. I show them the mental movie of the behavior they are doing and let them feel the negative emotions it generates for their people. For example, I will express to the animal how peeing on the rug makes his person very angry and disappointed. I put in as much detail

Chapter Four: Changing Behavior

as is needed and add body sensations, if I can. Then I show them an alternative behavior that generates positive emotion like going potty outside instead of in the house. I only focus on one behavior at a time, with one *Naughty* movie and one *Nice* movie. The sound track varies, with the emotional intensity increasing if appropriate. When they decide they would rather not get the negative emotion, a lot of times the animal will make a submissive gesture like licking their lips or breaking eye contact.

Using negative and positive emotion to change behavior is a process and it can take some time to be effective. Boomer had an unusual type of dog aggression. If another dog was walking towards him, he had no reaction. If a dog walked across his path he became aggressive, barking and lunging. He was gaining weight and wasn't getting the exercise he needed because his people were afraid to walk him. I showed him a mental movie of a generic dog crossing in front of him. His pupils would dilate and his breathing would get fast every time I showed him this visualization. He was feeling the urge to charge, even though there was not another dog present. The visualization alone was enough to trigger his aggressive response. I put gentle pressure on the **Magic Spot** to keep him focused and showed him the same movie about fifty times until he was completely bored with it and did not have an automatic physical reaction.

As that point, I added the emotional sound track. I showed him the *Naughty* movie (barking and lunging) coupled with his people being upset, sad and disappointed if he reacted to another dog. Then I showed him the *Nice* movie and let him feel how proud and happy they would be if he just watched a dog walk in front of him. These were very short and simple movies and I added some variety by showing him different dogs in different settings, but always with negative emotion for reacting and positive emotion for not reacting. We were able to work through a year's worth of dog encounters in less than twenty minutes. Boomer finally *got it*; he sighed deeply and lowered his head, the tension gone from his face. At that point, the idea of another dog walking in front of him was no more interesting than seeing a car drive by.

Of course, to make the change permanent, his people had to change their behavior as well. They had to mentally practice not reacting if they saw a dog that would be crossing in front of him. They needed to be prepared so they could remain calm enough to correct his behavior instead of making it worse. I suggested they go to a park and just sit in the car, watching dogs walk by so they could monitor their response to the stimulus, focus on keeping Boomer quiet and praise him for not reacting. That way, everyone would succeed. Eventually, they were able to sit on a bench with him showing no interest as dogs walked by and progress to walking towards the main sidewalk as other dogs crossed in front of them. Correcting this behavior didn't happen in one session and Boomer's people had to dedicate the time needed to make an effective change. Let compassion guide you and use both sides of your brain to come up with a workable solution to the problem. Make the effort to do it right.

What Animals Want

People often call me when they are at the end of their rope and can't think of anything other than removing the animal from the home. I always ask the people what outcome they want to see. Most would be brokenhearted to not have the animal in their lives. I never threaten animals, but if they are very resistant to changing a behavior, I will show them the result of being taken out of their home. I visualize what their life would be like in a noisy shelter with lots of other animals and little attention. I let them feel what a truly uncomfortable place it is. I show them living in a small cage with bars and let them feel the loss of freedom. I repeat this until they begin to accept that life as a possibility if they don't change. Then we begin coming to an agreement about what is acceptable and what isn't.

Changing behavior is often a negotiation and the animal has something they want from the humans in return. The whole point is for both partners to have a way to get their needs met. Animals desire simple, concrete things that influence their lives. I have never had an animal express that they would stop peeing on the carpet in exchange for world peace. I did have a cat show me he wanted a huge box of live mice in the living room if he wasn't allowed to go outside. This made his person laugh and she realized how important outside time was for him. She agreed to spend a few minutes outside with him every morning while she had coffee.

If they live in a household with other animals, sometimes the one who is acting out wants more one-on-one time with their person. This can be a few minutes a day of snuggling and focused attention, with no other people or animals in the room, going for a walk together or playing a special game. Ten minutes of undivided attention daily from their person is usually more valuable to animals than an hour once a week. Animals love routine. Other animals want more exercise or outside access. Sometimes, they want an animal or person to leave the home, which usually doesn't happen. Some want their person to be happier and generate more positive emotion (often true if the person is depressed). Overwhelmingly, they want to improve the relationship.

Occasionally, we reach a place where they can't compromise and they choose not to accept the change I ask for. I can try different bargaining chips and show different movies, but sometimes they won't acquiesce. I can't tell any animal or any person how to feel or change who they are. I cannot force my will, or by proxy, their person's will on them. At that point, I negotiate with the person for the best solution for the animal, one that keeps them safe, healthy and meets as many of their emotional needs as possible. Rarely, the solution comes to re-homing the animal or having the animal (usually a cat) living as an only animal by being restricted to one part of the house.

Too many people function on autopilot in their relationships with their animals, but by reading this book and doing the exercises, you have taken steps towards a more conscious partnership. You can touch your animal and use the information you receive to help keep them healthy. The words you use to describe your partner and your relationship have changed and you have reconnected with your right brain thinking skills. When combined with your left brain analytical abilities, your mental movies can help you change your behavior and your animals'. Creating expectations and enforcing boundaries has empowered you to take back your natural authority in the relationship. Most importantly, you have greatly increased your emotional acuity and can use positive and negative emotion to compassionately improve your partnerships. The next chapter will give you some examples of how to apply this knowledge to solve some common behavior challenges.

Chapter Five: Practical Examples

This section describes how I work through difficult behaviors. Some of these are major deal breakers and can result in the animal being re-homed and others are minor annoyances. These are not step-by-step recipes, but are examples of how to apply the concepts discussed in the first part of the book. They are models that you can adapt to your specific circumstances. Most of these examples are for dog behavior, but the techniques work with all animals and there is a section just about cats. There is also useful information about moving with animals (which is an excellent place to apply your animal communication skills) and what to do if your animal goes missing. Feel free to read all of the examples or just those that apply to your situation.

- Inappropriate elimination
- Separation anxiety
- Stop barking
- Ignore
- Cats
- Moving
- Missing animals

Inappropriate Elimination

Potty issues are one of the most common things people call me about. This is a serious boundary violation and may be a matter of life and death for the animal. Inappropriate elimination is one of the main reasons animals end up in shelters. Sometimes there is no quick fix to this behavior because it can consist of a combination of physical, mental and emotional factors and requires some very focused action from the humans.

There can be many physical reasons for not going potty in the right place. This can be caused by everything from stress, food intolerance, illness or physical pain. Cats that pee on the carpet may have a medical condition like crystals in their urine or urinary tract infections that need to be treated with a change of diet or a course of antibiotics. Pay attention to the physical clues your animal gives you. Are they eating or drinking more or less than usual? Does their posture look different? Has their behavior changed toward another animal or person? Sometimes I can tell if a cat has kidney problems by smelling their breath. I am pretty immune to stinky cat breath, but I am good at detecting the scent of ammonia. This is a huge red flag and indicates the cat needs immediate medical attention.

The next thing to consider is the animal's action from their perspective. Are they violating this boundary because they are literally *pissed off* about something like another animal, new baby or change in routine? Is your job or relationship affecting them? Is the litter box an EPA Superfund site? If an animal's territorial boundary is being violated by other animals, they can start marking. Sometimes you can get a clue about what is going on by looking at where they go. If a dog or cat sprays a vertical surface, it is usually about territory or dominance. If they go in a hidden spot, it can mean they are ill. If an animal squats right in front of you, it can mean a painful bladder infection (they need to go NOW) or it is an act of defiance. If you have been practicing moving

Chapter Five: Practical Examples

energy through their body and notice a change from normal, trust that information and get them to the vet.

The problem is, once an animal has marked a surface, it can be very difficult to get the scent out. Just because you can't smell it doesn't mean your animal can't. If they get even a whiff of urine from a specific spot, it is giving them an invitation to go there again. It also gives another animal permission to mark over that place. One of the most important steps in breaking this behavior is thorough cleaning. This is a huge part of actualizing your expectation and enforcing a very essential boundary. Soap and water, vinegar and even steam cleaning don't get all of the scent out of carpet. There are a variety of enzymatic cleaners that will completely break down urine and feces and remove the scent. Go buy a gallon, right now.

Urine spots glow under a black light. Bite the bullet and get the black light when you pick up the enzymatic cleaner. Turn off the regular lights and turn on the black light. I have had people do this and immediately decide to rip out the carpet because it looked like stars on a dark night. Even old spots will show up under the black light, so the first time you do this, you have to treat *everything*. Really soak all the spots with the cleaner. You also have to treat the carpet pad, sub floor and any woodwork next to the area as well. Do not neglect the cleaning step, it is crucial to your success.

Once you have eliminated any scent cues from the environment, treated any medical problems and taken a good look at stresses your animal is experiencing, it is time to work on behavior. If you come home and find poop on the carpet, you have three choices: you can sigh heavily and just clean it up, get mad at your friend and use too much force (potentially damaging your partnership) or you can use this as a training opportunity and address the behavior using some of your best human skills. It is not true that you have to catch them in the act. Dogs and cats are not like goldfish, they have good memories for emotional events and you are going to make inappropriate elimination an emotional event.

Say you have three dogs, about the same size, and you come home from work to a wet spot on the floor. Take each dog, one at a time to the spot and point at it. Do not rub their face in it, this is rude and abusive. All that does is make them fear you and they will completely shut you off. Say something like, "Did you do this? This is totally UN-AC-CEPT-A-BLE! I will not tolerate this disgusting behavior in my house! Do not EVER do this again! I will not allow you to disrespect my property and you will NOT pee on my carpet!" This is the **Unacceptable Speech** and it is a very effective tool to change your animal's behavior. Keep the diatribe about how you feel (angry, disrespected, frustrated…) and put some real energy into it. You are talking about the behavior and emphasizing the spot on the carpet, not saying mean things to the dog. Every dog is equally responsible for this boundary violation because they may have marked over the first dog's transgression, so repeat the process, appropriately adjusting the intensity for each animal. After you have expressed your disapproval to all of the dogs, get out the enzymatic cleaner and thoroughly clean up the mess.

Giving the correction is about your emotions in response to their action. The exact words aren't important as long as you are expressing how you feel and aren't belittling the animal. Does your dog understand what you are saying to him? No. Does he care that you are very upset? Yes. Remember the Monster episode with the wine? Don't underestimate the power of forceful emotion, appropriately applied. One good, emotionally relevant correction is worth fifty ineffective ones. Take advantage of trainable moments and don't just deal with the mess without actively working towards a solution. Because dogs are social animals, they can all work together to please you. Some dogs are very good at being the cop, policing the behavior of other dogs.

This type of emotional correction also works with cats. Cats are very sensitive to negative emotion, but you won't get the guilty look from a cat (actually more submissive than guilty in dogs). Showing them the boundary violation, expressing your displeasure with the behavior and using negative emotion can be very effective in changing a cat's behavior, but they are not social animals, so don't expect them to police each other.

There are a few exceptions for using the **Unacceptable Speech**. The first is with puppies, especially very young ones under three months of age. When you are house training a puppy, start gently and always put the emphasis on the positive emotion. If you take the puppy outside consistently after she wakes up, has play time or after she eats, she will become aware of the physical sensation in her body and eventually understand how to respond to it. Use the same verbal prompt (it isn't a command at this point) and shower her with praise when she does what you expect. As a puppy gets older (four to six months), but is still having accidents in the house, you can use Unacceptable in a gentle way to show that the behavior is inappropriate. This is not about reward and punishment, threats, bribes or intimidation. You set a boundary and get your animal to respect it. You are teaching her good behavior and setting the foundation for a solid partnership by getting her to work with you. The corrections can become more intense if needed, but you can't undo the negative emotions you create by reacting in an uncontrolled manner. Everything you do with young animals or a recently adopted one should be about building trust and respect. Don't assume a new adult dog is housebroken. Supervision is essential. Keep an eye on him until you feel like you can trust him or keep him physically confined to one area of the house.

It takes some effort to visually differentiate inside and outside and it is helpful to imagine this from the dog's point of view. How does the experience of being inside differ from being outside? You need to make the distinction very clear and apply negative emotion to the inside visualization and a large amount of positive emotion to the outside image. Be patient and consistent. Potty training can be a real challenge in the winter when the snow is higher than your puppy's head. Use your talented left brain and do everything you can (have a regular routine, shovel the patio, put a coat on him) to help him go potty outside then cheerfully praise him when he does. Using absorbent pads is confusing for puppies. This gives him the idea that it is okay to potty in the house and asks him to make a distinction between the pad and the throw rug. Some dogs, like Italian Greyhounds are notoriously challenging to house train. They have no fur, virtually no body fat and shiver if it is below 75 degrees. You may have better luck using an indoor dog litter box if you live in a cooler climate.

Another exception to showing strong emotion is working with older animals that may have become incontinent or senile. If they start having accidents, it may be that their bladder is weaker, or they may have had a stroke or spinal injury that keeps them from receiving appropriate signals when their bladder is full. A dog that has back or joint problems may find it painful to get up and go outside, for example. You may have to change your schedule so the dog doesn't go as long without potty breaks or change their physical environment and make it easier for them to move around by installing a larger doggie door or a ramp. Pain medication can be helpful and there are medications that help with bladder control. Work with your vet to make life easier for both you and your older animal.

You don't have to just accept that your dog is old and you can't change a behavior once it starts. You can teach old dogs new tricks, or at least remind them of the tricks they already know. Communicating through visualization and emotion is effective even with deaf or blind animals. After you have treated any medical problems, you need to re-potty-train your dog, just like you would a puppy. Again, a schedule can give you a lot of structure. Let him outside, give the command "Go potty," feel the sensation of having a full bladder in your own body and then the relief when you finally get to go. When he does go potty in the right place, show lots of positive emotion and give him a bunch of praise. Be enthusiastic, and if you're not, at least pretend that you are.

If your older animal has an accident in the house, give him some focused negative emotion in a gentle way, reminding him that is not appropriate behavior. I'm not saying you need to yell at your older animal, just review the house rules. You are still expressing disapproval, but in a less dramatic way. You may need to practice this before correcting the dog. You need to re-establish the boundary about where he should relieve himself. Some animals get to the place where they can't control their bladder or bowels because of age or disease. If they are aware of the fact that they have accidents, it can be very distressing to them and cause a lot of suffering. This is always one of the things I look for when it comes to making an end-of-life decision, if the animal is losing their dignity and it makes their life miserable.

Not wanting to go potty can also be a problem, but is much less common than going in the wrong place. I worked with a lady who had an extremely constipated dog. He had developed a condition where his bowel was stretched and misshapen. The woman tried every kind of diet and supplement available with little or no effect and was facing a very expensive and difficult surgery for her friend.

The dog showed me pictures of his previous owner leaving him alone for several days and then punishing him very harshly for soiling the house. This abuse had left the dog phobic about leaving poop anywhere. Relieving a full bladder or bowel is an easy feeling to transmit to a dog or cat. He understood that going potty would feel good after we went over it a few times and then we worked on the phobia a bit. As is common in rescue animals, he was very devoted to the woman and really wanted to please her. I told him how he never had to go back to where he came from and then visualized him hiding poops all over the yard. I made it feel like a really exciting game, like hunting Easter eggs, and showed him how much joy his person would have finding them. She called me a couple months later and said the dog hadn't had any problems since and that she was very happy doing poop patrol.

Separation Anxiety

A lot of dogs (and some cats) act out when their people leave the house. This is a pretty common complaint, but I only see one or two animals a year that truly have separation anxiety. They essentially have a panic attack, their heart rate and breathing go through the roof and a lot of times, they salivate. Some don't act out at all because their body is so stressed they can't function. These animals really suffer and they can be helped greatly with medication.

The other animals that are described as having separation anxiety are the result of conditioned behaviors practiced daily with their people. The first thing I ask the person is if they like their job. This always surprises them and the vast majority say they don't. If you don't like what you do, you wake up to the alarm with trepidation. As soon as the coffee kicks in, you begin to review the tape loop playing in your head about how your boss is a jerk, your co-workers are idiots and the fridge is a science experiment gone wrong. You play these scenes over and over, generating huge amounts of negative emotions. You are much more involved with these mental movies than what you are actually doing as you get ready for work, so you function on autopilot. By the time you leave, you are tense, unhappy and self-absorbed. Your animal companion is very aware of this tsunami of negativity and they also know how emotionally wounded you are when you come home. They don't want you to go to the place that makes you sad. They don't understand why you need to work (mainly to buy food and toys for them), they just know that you are not happy about it.

When you leave the house in a dramatic emotional scene, what they really want is for you to say, "You're right. This is a stupid way to spend my life and it is much more important to take you to the park." Animals will use all of their tools to manipulate you with the hope that you won't leave or will at least give them a lot of very emotionally charged attention before you do. Some people have leaving rituals that rival the death scene in a tragic opera for the amount of drama they produce, with both partners passionately playing their parts. Do some **Automatic Writing** to sort through these difficult emotions.

Your routine behaviors are effective as they get you out the door, but you have disconnected a large part of your brain. It would be interesting to record what someone says to an animal with separation anxiety as they get ready to leave for work. Words like *leaving, going* and expressions like *I'm going to miss you*, and *I wish I didn't have to go*, would probably dominate the very one-sided conversation. Tune into the words gushing from your lips. Where is your focus? Saying, "I'm leaving in about fifteen minutes. After work tonight, I'm going to stop by the dry cleaner and the bank and pick up some groceries. I'll probably be home about seven," is not helpful. The only thing your dog understands is one word, *leaving*. To the dog that means *I am abandoning you* and they go right into their deepest fear.

Your observant and emotionally aware animal companion knows you are leaving long before you walk out the door. You, the center of his universe, are leaving. Leaving him. Just because you have come home a thousand times doesn't mean your dog isn't feeling the same fear and abandonment as when he was taken away from his mother as a pup. Remembered emotion is just as powerful as real-time emotion. Animals that have had some kind of trauma often have a low level of anxiety that is always present. If they are in a stressful situation, even if it is only vaguely similar to what they have experienced, they often overreact. Their pump is already primed. Their physical response can be completely out of proportion to the emotional input.

Separation anxiety affects animals physically; they go on heightened alert and it raises their general stress level, making it harder for them to relax. I believe it also makes them age faster. Dogs that are worriers tend to have bodies that feel older than their chronological age. I worked with two Golden Retrievers who perfectly illustrated this point.

Chapter Five: Practical Examples

Alexi, the male, was a lovable lug who just wanted to play ball with the boy in his family. He didn't have a care in the world and he looked and acted like he was six. His sister Amber was a worrier. She was anxious about the woman's new husband (who didn't like dogs) and the woman had also changed jobs and had a different schedule. Amber worried that she wasn't coming home. Her eyes were cloudy, her muzzle was grey and her energy felt like she was about eleven. They were both eight when I visited them. They had similar genetics and environment, but Amber's anxiety had a huge impact on her body compared to her brother's.

Leaving your animal companions in a huge emotional scene contributes to stress and anxiety for both of you. This is a small but steady drain on your energy. Standing in the driveway, waving to your dog (who has jumped on the couch to look out the window) while you wipe away tears is not a good way to start your day. Choose something better for both of you. Decide what behaviors you want to see and take action to create them. Do the **"if this, then that"** mental movie test, visualize your typical leave-taking and play the emotional soundtrack. How do you feel about what you are viewing? Do you feel like a rock has been dropped into your stomach? Now imagine telling your friend, "I'll be back," (you can say this in your *Terminator* voice, your dog won't care) then walking out the door and starting your day. No tears, no sad eyes, just a normal part of your life. Which movie feels better to you?

Practice this visualization when you are not with your animal. This will help you take the emphasis off the leaving and put it where it belongs, on the returning.

- Picture yourself getting ready to go in a calm, unemotional way. Tune into how you feel and what you are saying, avoiding emotional trigger words. You can do the **Moving energy down and up** exercise or the **Right Brain Breathing** to help stay grounded and keep from being caught up in your own negative emotions.

- Visualize calmly picking up your things and telling your dog verbally, visually and emotionally what she wants to hear, "I love you and I will come home for you." Don't picture yourself leaving. Put all of the physical, mental and emotional emphasis of this mental movie on coming home.

- Picture yourself returning. You walk up to the door, turn the key, then greet your friend. Play the soundtrack of how glad you are to see her and how you look forward to a relaxing evening. Do this in a composed, non-reactive way. You are showing your animal what to expect.

- Mentally practice walking out the door in a relaxed and composed way. No trauma, no drama. Rehearse this scene until you can control your physical and emotional response. Leaving your home in the morning should be no more eventful than walking out of the grocery store.

- Compare how you feel when you watch this mental movie with how you feel about your typical leave-taking. Which step of the **Emotional Staircase** are you on? Are you moving upward to more positive emotions or are you slipping down into negativity?

Review this movie as many times as it takes for you to believe you can do this. Mentally rehearse what you will say, do and feel. Break your leaving ritual down into small, clear steps. Remember you are the writer, director and main actor

Chapter Five: Practical Examples

in this story, so make it something that you want to see every day.

Denial is a not a river in Egypt and if something generates large amounts of strong emotion, chances are it will not change by itself. Separation anxiety is a deeply codependent behavior and one of the hardest to change because it generates a mix of positive and negative emotions for both parties. Many people don't want to look at the root cause of their animal's bad behavior because it means changing some very ingrained patterns. The animal shows you parts of yourself that you may not want to acknowledge, like what you expect from relationships, how you define your purpose or areas in your life that aren't meeting your emotional needs. **Automatic Writing** will help you answer some of these questions for yourself. This may be challenging for you and it will take practice. Create an expectation about your own behavior and notice when leaving your animal starts to produce fewer negative emotions. You have opportunities to improve this behavior several days a week so use them.

If an animal has been traumatized from being returned to a shelter and readopted, for example, I will "prove" to the animal that the mental movie I show them is true; their person always comes back after they leave. You can do this with a friend or family member, someone the dog is comfortable with, as your helper. Review your mental movies about returning. Have the helper sit with the dog and put gentle pressure on the **Magic Spot** on their head while they mentally picture you returning. Pick up your keys, replay the mental movie of your return, tell your dog you will be back and walk out the door. Do this as unemotionally as possible and avoid saying trigger words. The helper is repeating your words and visualizing you returning, but they are not trying to comfort the dog, they are just reminding the dog that you will be back. When you walk in after a couple of minutes, the dog is overjoyed. The mental story has become reality! Greet the dog calmly, trying to not get him overly excited.

    Practice this several times in a day so you can both build new patterns. Repeat the visualization of returning and then walk out, with the helper interacting with the dog a little less each time. Add in other parts of your leaving routine, like opening the garage or starting the car, building in small, incremental steps. Your goal is to actually drive away and be gone for fifteen to twenty minutes. You may not be able to progress to this level in one session but keep working towards it. The hardest part is going to be keeping your own emotions in check. Some people see this as being unscrupulous on the part of the humans. I am not trying to deceive the dog in any way, the objective is to give their story a different ending and replace fear and anxiety with reassurance. After doing this exercise a few times, the animal often looks much less stressed. Many people tell me the dog is more relaxed as they get ready to leave and generally seems more at ease. Keep building on success and make a commitment to the new routines you are creating.

    Safe and secure are great feelings to send your animal and can be a very important soundtrack for your movie of returning. Think about a time you felt secure. Really put yourself into that memory, really feel it in your body. You will probably sigh and feel your shoulders relax when you recall this feeling. This is the emotional opposite of worry. Visualize the coming home movie throughout the day and send these emotions to your dog while you are away. Let him know that you love him and will always come home. Sometimes it is useful to give the animal a job to do. I tell Monster to get hair on the couch when I am gone. You can tell a dog, "Guard the house until I come home" and then praise him for doing a good job if you were not burglarized. If you were burglarized, you do have something to worry about.

If you feel yourself slipping back into the old, overly emotional leaving routine, stop what you are doing and identify how you feel. Do the mental movie test and decide which option feels better to you at that moment, the old pattern or the new one you are trying to create? Remind yourself why you are making this change and renew your commitment. Catch yourself when you say something like, "I hate my job and wish I didn't have to go in today," and shift your attention back to buttering your toast (you might even become aware that you just absent-mindedly fed half a piece to your dog). Praise your animal when you see improvement and acknowledge your effort towards building a more positive relationship. This is a correction that takes a lot of awareness on the human's part. Improvement may be gradual, but it is worth the time and energy.

Stop Barking

Just like we like to talk, dogs like to bark. Barking varies quite a bit by breed and individual. Some dogs rarely bark and some rarely stop. Barking can be a hard thing to correct, because it happens a lot when you aren't around. Start by discouraging barking when you are home, and then work on it when you aren't. If you have allowed your dog to bark relentlessly, this is going to be a challenge.

Alerting us when someone is coming is an essential job that dogs have done for thousands of years. Our human world has changed dramatically since we domesticated canines and their instincts haven't kept pace. There are so many things in the environment that dogs can bark at and barking can quickly become problematic if you don't establish some boundaries. This is something you can change to some extent, but you will probably not be able to completely extinguish it. Become aware of the situations where your dog barks. Sometimes it is a sign of boredom or frustration and dogs that don't get enough exercise or attention are prone to be barkers. Sending them to doggy daycare one or two days a week can be very useful in curbing this behavior. They can run and play and bark all they want and then when they come home, they are tired. A tired dog is a quiet dog.

To the dog, telling him "Don't bark!" or "No barking!" is ambiguous and confusing, kind of like saying "Don't breathe." Be precise in the words you use. When you say, "No barking," your focus is on the barking, not the stopping of the barking. You want the dog to "Stop barking," so tell him that in those words and expect it to happen. The more you yell at him with nonspecific emotion, the less authority you have and you are just barking back at him. The worst thing you can do is pick up your small dog when she is yapping her head off while trying to deal with the person at the door. People often unintentionally reward the behavior they are trying to correct. Become aware of your actions and stop doing this. Remember that if you get into an emotional struggle with your animal, they win every time. You have to out think them, so make a plan.

It is hard for a dog to bark when sitting or lying down. This is another one of those places where basic obedience training is useful. If your dog barks when someone comes to the door, give the command "Sit" first, then the command "Stop barking" and expect him to do it. Visualize him sitting with his mouth closed. He is intently watching and listening to see what is happening, but he is not barking.

Timeout can be a very useful tool to limit barking in the house. Timeout is effective because you physically remove the animal from the situation instead of letting it escalate. Visualize someone knocking at the door and your dog going crazy. Picture yourself answering the door and telling the person to wait a moment. Give the dog the command "Stop barking" and when she doesn't, say something like, "Do you need a timeout?" Take your dog (it is okay to pick up a small dog in this case and easier if you have a leash on a larger dog) away from the door and put her in a small, quiet room like the bathroom or laundry room. You have planned ahead and prepared the area, making sure there is nothing she can destroy or that could hurt her (many cleaning products are dangerous to animals so be sure she can't get in the cabinets). There are no toys, treats, food, water or blankets in the room. Turn out the lights. She is going to stay in timeout for ten minutes. Visualize this procedure several times so you know what actions you are going to do and then set up opportunities to practice. Write out this script in your journal.

Timeout is not about punishment; it is about isolation. The dog would much rather see what is going on than be in a boring little room. When you take the dog to timeout, don't scold or reprimand her for barking. The best thing you can do is not talk to her at all. You need to "stop barking" as well and not add emotional fuel to her fire. When you let her out after ten minutes, all is forgiven. Do not hold a grudge against her or treat her any differently. If she starts barking again, she gets another timeout.

Timing is essential here so practice mentally and be prepared to act out your part. The dog barks a couple times, and then you give the command "Stop barking." It is much easier to stop the action as it starts instead of letting it go on for five minutes and becoming emotionally worked up. Timeout is the consequence for ignoring this command. Make timeout predictable and boring, so the dog chooses to avoid it by not barking. If she stops barking, she can stay in the room. If she continues to bark, she is removed. Respond quickly and effectively. If you have to stop and think about what to do in that circumstance, the dog will continue to enthusiastically bark her head off, making it that much harder to get her to stop.

Bring your mental movie into the real world and practice. Pick a weekend when you don't have much going on. Enlist several friends to come to your home at different times and ring your doorbell. Tell them what is going on and have a plan about how you will respond. They ring the bell, the dog barks and you give the command, "Stop barking." The dog isn't going to recognize what you want her to do, so she keeps barking. Give the "Do you need a timeout?" prompt and put her in the other room. If you let her out and she barks at the person, give the command "Stop barking" and put her back in timeout. Some dogs catch on to this very quickly and you will only have to do it a few times, others take longer. Do this exercise several times in one day and also practice a day or two later. If she stops barking when you say, "Stop barking," reward her with praise and let her stay in the room.

This is an all or nothing correction; you get very little benefit if you do not make a full commitment to improving the behavior every time it happens. Everyone in the house has to correct the behavior the same way, so communicate what you are doing and why. Decide beforehand how much barking you will allow, the command you will give and the consequences (positive and negative) you will enforce. If you are consistent about giving timeout and then just ignore the barking a couple of times, you communicate to the dog that you aren't serious about the change and she doesn't have to do it. There has to be a predictable consequence for the dog's action.

If you have multiple dogs, barking is usually worse. The dogs feed off of each other's excitement and egg each other on. Start doing timeout with the worst offender, the dog that starts the barking or persists the longest. Conduct some experiments by having people knock and removing a different dog each time. Observe which combination produces the least amount of barking. Adding a physical barrier like a baby gate that keeps the dogs from being right at the door can make it easier to put them in timeout. Sometimes the simplest solution is the most effective.

If you are in a situation where the dog barks when you are not home, get them to understand the command "Stop barking" first. This helps because you create an expectation of their conduct and establish a boundary. Make sure the dog's emotional and physical needs are being met. Practice the visualization of your dog spending his day in silence. If you have to, use a device like an ultrasonic bark collar to keep your dog quiet. Find a system that uses sound or vibration, but not electrical shock. There are some that are not triggered by another dog's barking. I really don't like any of these and only recommend them as a last resort. You have a responsibility to be as humane to the animal as possible and still respect your neighbors and solve the problem.

Ignore

Animals react emotionally in emotional situations. Guess what? So do people. *Ignore* can be a very useful idea to teach any animal. It is not a natural response for animals and most have to learn to not react to an emotional trigger. If you set a bowl of cold, lumpy oatmeal in front of me, I would turn away and pretend it was not there. I wouldn't start poking at it with my spoon saying, "Ew, yuck! Get that disgusting gruel away from me! I'm not going to eat that!" That is the opposite of *Ignore*. You can visualize your animal (and yourself) not reacting, giving them the emotional combination of non-interest and boredom. *Ignore* is a form of non-acknowledgement and the attitude is "Who cares?" The person or animal is still aware of the stimulus, but does not respond to it.

Practicing *Ignore* is a good way to deal with annoying behaviors like begging or when an animal tries to manipulate you, by dropping a toy on your lap, for example. Ignoring is very different from being mindless. It is a deliberate action in which you are fully aware of the behavior, but you do not acknowledge it in any way. You don't look at the animal, talk to them or engage them. You think to yourself, "Nope, no dogs here. I don't even have a dog." *Ignore* lasts until the behavior stops, but no longer. You are not giving your friend the cold shoulder indefinitely; you just don't let him push your buttons. This is very different from absent-mindedly brushing the dog's paw off your arm ten times and then exploding when you have finally had enough. *Ignore* gives you the backbone to effectively stand up to pushback and change your relationships for the better.

I have taught *Ignore* to all types of animals as well as people. This can be useful if you have a dog that likes to chase your cats in a recreational way, for example. You can teach them to ignore each other. Visualize them walking past each other and add the emotion of ignoring. Vary the setting, so they get the idea to always ignore each other. A lot of times, the cat is equally responsible as the dog for this game. The cat will entice the dog and the dog will respond.

Chapter Five: Practical Examples

You can't make animals like each other and "be friends," but you can establish some household tranquility. You have to be prepared to take immediate action to stop the chase game as soon as it starts, giving negative emotion to both parties. It is even better if you can prevent the rodeo from starting in the first place by noticing how your animals interact. Start playing the *Ignore* movie as soon as they begin antagonizing each other and separate or distract them. Play the mental movie of them ignoring each other so often that everyone gets bored with it and chooses to do something else.

You help your animal learn to ignore something when you are in the present moment and aware of what you are focusing on. A man who ran on a popular trail had a dog that would submissively roll over on her back every time another dog approached. This meant he had to stop running, which was very frustrating to him. He started wearing a heart rate monitor for training and noticed that any time he saw a dog, even at a distance of a hundred yards, his heart rate would increase. He figured out on his own that he was partly responsible for his dog's actions because he was so focused on other dogs. The more he could ignore other dogs, the less reactive his dog was. This was a huge revelation for him and he became very conscious of monitoring his heart rate, noticing if it was increasing from exertion or apprehension. He was able to change his dog's behavior enough that they could enjoy exercising together.

In the above example, the man had a very important role to play. He had to practice *Ignore* by not getting tense when he saw another dog. A leash connects your observational brain directly to your dog's reactive one. If it is another dog, a stroller, balloons, sprinklers or anything else the dog reacts to, you will use your highly developed visual acuity and BFHB to seek it out in the environment. When you find it, you fixate on it and go into fight or flight mode. You tense up (especially in your neck and shoulders) and also tighten your grip on the leash or even wrap it around your hand because you know he is going to act like an idiot. You have very effectively alerted the dog that you feel threatened and he understands that you, his person, are in jeopardy. He is instantly ready to defend you to his last breath. As the other dog approaches, they have had plenty of time to trash talk each other and get all worked up. Of course they get into it, what else can they do?

The more you can willfully ignore a stimulus, the less volatile your dog will be. Here is a simple little exercise to help you understand the information you send through the leash (or reins, it works with horses, too). This assumes that your dog can heel. There is no point doing this exercise if the dog can't walk next to you at a comfortable pace. Becoming aware of what you are doing physically affects you mentally and emotionally. Focus on your hand. **Hold the leash** lightly yet firmly using two fingers and your thumb in a pinch grip. Notice the exact moment you put your full hand on the leash and check in with your body and your emotions. The outside of your hand (through the pinky finger) is the strongest part of your grip. When you fixate on *The Threat* and shift from lightly holding the leash to *The Death Grip*, you transmit your tension and anxiety directly to your animal. The dog is not objectively thinking, "Hey, that dog looks friendly; mom is just overreacting again," he responds to the emotional signals you are sending and is ready to take action.

Avoidance is not ignoring. Sometimes people go out of their way to not encounter whatever it is the dog reacts to. This could be shunning certain places or walking at odd times. It can be fun to walk your dog at night (depending on your neighborhood), but this is different than changing your work schedule and walking your dog at two a.m. so you won't encounter another dog. This might be a matter of picking your battles, but it can also signal that you are entrenched in the problem, believing your own stories and letting the dog rule your life. You have to acknowledge your part in this pattern and intentionally change your emotions and behavior.

Some people tell me there is no way to restrain the dog when he reacts because their dog is "too strong." This is another example of being stuck in the problem and not looking for a real solution. Have you ever seen a dog show on TV? Huge dogs, who are completely surrounded by other dogs, wear collars and leashes that are little more than jewelry. If someone has a dog that is reactive on a leash, the first thing they do is buy a choke chain or a pinch collar and when that doesn't work, they buy a bigger one. This is like an arms race in which only one side gets to buy hardware. It is much easier to buy something than to look at how your actions contribute to your animal's behavior.

Instead of an ineffective pinch collar try a Gentle Leader. This is kind of like a halter; part of it fits over the dog's nose and a strap goes high and tight behind their ears. You lead them from under the chin, so it takes their body out of the equation and gives you a lot more physical control. Because of the way a Gentle Leader is designed, they don't work well on dogs with short muzzles, like Pugs, but they do work for most dogs. When a dog pulls against a Gentle Leader, the top strap gives them a headache; the more they resist, the stronger the headache gets. When they stop pulling, the headache stops. There is no strength-against-strength contest and it doesn't lead to meanness. This is more effective than a pinch collar or choke chain because the dog's actions directly influence the duration and intensity of the correction.

I tell clients to take their dog into the pet supply store if possible, and have one of the salespeople fit a Gentle Leader for them. It is not intuitive how it goes on and it takes some trial and error to get it adjusted correctly. The piece that goes behind the dog's ears is tight; you can barely slide one finger under it. The first time you put it on at home, all you do is hold the leash. This is a new sensation for the dog and she will resist it. Dogs often jump and scream and fall on the ground and paw at their head and whine. It can be quite a show. Do not cave in and take it off just because she hates it. She is acting like a nut because it is working. The longest I've seen a dog resist a Gentle Leader was about ten minutes; most only go three or four. Just hold the leash and don't respond. You are not giving the correction, the equipment is. All of this resistance gives her a nasty headache. When she has had enough, she will calm down. That's when you give lots of praise and maybe a treat and take the Gentle Leader off.

The second time you get it out, things will be different. The dog knows what it is and many times they play keep away or try to steal it from you. Put the Gentle Leader on and start walking, expecting the dog to walk right next to your side at the pace you set. Most dogs will balk at first, but the headache will motivate them pretty quickly. There is no tugging and pulling on your part. You just walk and allow her to keep up with you. You can give the command, "Heel" but don't give any correction with the leash. Hold it lightly with two fingers and your thumb so you are not tempted to pull on it. You walk at a steady pace, not aimlessly meandering from one sniffing spot to another. If the dog resists, just keep walking. Your momentum, coupled with the Gentle Leader will convince her that walking with you is the best option. When you see the behavior you want, praise her.

Chapter Five: Practical Examples

Your dog is just as responsible for your fitness as you are for hers. Being able to walk at a steady pace is good for both of you and a lot more fun than a tug and pull contest.

Cats

Cats are our least likely domesticated animals. Dogs and horses are very social and are willing to give some responsibility over to the group leader. They are naturally inclined to work in partnership with humans, doing a variety of jobs for us. Cats are solitary hunters and their only job has been killing rodents, which they are extremely good at. They are not interested in hierarchy or cooperation. Cats really love their person and are very loyal, but it takes more effort to change their behavior because they don't see us as leaders. The thing I love about cats is they are all unique, complete individuals and it is impossible to make generalizations about them.

Having another cat plunked down in the middle of their domain is very stressful for them and they have no concept of "sharing." I used to do a lot of house sitting and I would take my old cat with me. I would get all the cats together in the bathroom and have a catnip party. I made piles for them to eat and I rubbed it on their heads. Some got so stoned they couldn't walk. When they finally recovered enough to notice there was a new cat, they didn't really care that much. I never had any problem leaving my cat with other cats. This wasn't some kind of deep feline bonding experience, but the catnip short circuits their territorial defense reactions, and as a result negative patterns don't get started. Catnip only affects about three quarters of cats. It is a genetic trait and can't be changed. Even if you have one cat that is not affected, cats are tribal and they will usually go along with what the other cats do.

Cats can display some terrible behavior when they feel like their territory is being invaded. Even if your cat never goes outside, they think they own what they can see from the window. Monster goes into ninja assassin mode if she sees a cat half a block away. Cats, dogs and wild animals can all be seen as invaders. If a cat that has normally been good about using their litter box starts marking, they may be trying to claim their territory. You can help them with this by chasing off other animals and not encouraging them to come near your home in the first place. Feeding neighborhood cats is a kind thing to do, but it can backfire if it stresses out your cats. If you have free roaming dogs or cats that hang around, scare them off by putting a couple pennies or small rocks in a soda can and taping it shut. If you see the other animal, throw the can near them (not at them) with the intent that they leave and don't come back. Taking some of your cat's used litter and spreading it around the perimeter of your outside space can give other animals the message the area has been claimed and they should stay out. You have to reapply this every couple of weeks or after it rains. You may not have to do this forever, just until the other animals change their patterns and stop coming around.

Cats can also turn on their companion cats if they feel invaded. A friend had two cats that were very close and often slept together. One day Jill started attacking Jack and they couldn't even be in the same room together without snarling and hissing. I dialoged with them to help figure out what set them off. Jill was sitting in a basement window and a dog came up to it. She got very defensive and when Jack jumped up to see what the problem was, she felt like she was being attacked from two sides and tore into him. He became a threat and she acted like she didn't even know him. I advised my friend to separate them for a couple of days, giving each

Chapter Five: Practical Examples

their own food, water and litter box. Once they calmed down, she could start to slowly reintroduce them. She had to practice ignoring their negative interactions and praise both of them when they were tolerating each other. It took about a month, but they reestablished their friendship and stopped fighting.

Some cats (like Monster) are anti-social to the point that they are offended other cats exist on the planet, let alone in their house. In a multiple cat home, at least one cat believes she is Alexander the Great and has command over the entire known world. She will use every tool available to guard what she considers to be hers. This cat will position herself in a way that blocks access to desirable resources like food, water or the litter box. You walk by and wonder why the cat is sitting in the middle of the hall. She doesn't look particularly comfortable or relaxed, but her eyes are half closed. This is resource guarding and that cat is trash talking the other cats to keep them away from her stuff. A lot of times, it is very hard for humans to recognize this behavior, partly because cat faces are not as expressive as dog faces and we miss most of the subtle communication that goes on between cats. It is also because people are much more tolerant of eccentric behavior in cats than dogs. Pay attention to how your animals interact with each other.

Even if you just have two cats, one cat is guarding resources and the other cat is stressed about it. If a cat is prevented from using the litter box, it causes a lot of strain on their kidneys and can lead to very unpleasant behaviors such as spraying or not using the box at all. Having several boxes in a row in the basement may work well for you, but not so well for your cats as one cat can block access to all of them. The more water bowls and litter boxes you have and the more spread out they are, the better chance you have of avoiding some awful cat behavior. A good rule of thumb is to have one litter box for each cat plus an extra one. If you live in a multilevel house, have litter boxes on each floor. Yes, you will have to scoop them and be clever about how you hide them, but your BFHB will help you overcome this challenge. There is no way to stop a cat from guarding resources, but you can intervene when you notice the behavior by getting that cat to move from her spot or distracting her with play. Practicing the *Ignore* visualization can also be useful. Picture the cats walking past each other and not reacting. You have to put some effort into changing cat behavior. Cats are smart, but they have a lousy work ethic and are not interested in changing their behavior to please us.

Cat behavior often becomes ritualized and they will do the same thing in the same way. If your cat has developed a habit that is impossible to break, like it will only urinate on newspapers, you need to seriously think inside the box. Shredded newspapers make a fine cat litter. Sometimes, cats will only go on things like plastic, at which point you could just use a plastic bag as a liner in the box and add litter to absorb the urine. The more cats you have, the more litter options you will need. Some cats spend all day outside and then rush in to use the litter box. Some cats love self-cleaning litter boxes, others won't get near them. Some cats will not go in a box after another cat has used it, others don't mind at all. Some cats hate using a box with a cover or one that is placed in a corner. They like to walk around and pick the best position. There are even round litter boxes that some cats really like. You are better off experimenting with box size (big boxes for big cats, for example) and placement rather than different types or brands of litter. Changing from one type of litter to another should be a gradual process. Don't do it if you don't have to.

Chapter Five: Practical Examples

The qualities that you may be interested in with cat litter are not necessarily the same as what your cat is interested in. Litters that have clumping agents, dust reduction and odor control are often laced with chemicals that are not good for your cat. Your cat has small lungs and stirs up these chemicals every time she steps in the box. The fewer chemicals, the better. Monster approaches litter kicking like it is an Olympic sport. She has two boxes, a normal one that is placed inside of a very large plastic storage container to keep the litter in. Be creative about litter solutions and make access easy, especially for older cats that may have difficulty climbing into a higher box. Think of a really yucky gas station restroom. That feeling of revulsion is similar to how cats experience a dirty litter box. They don't even want to touch it and would much rather go on the clean carpet, especially if they can smell urine from a past incident. Scooping the litter box is not my favorite part of living with felines, but it takes a lot less time than getting cat hair off my clothes and is much more beneficial to our relationship. Just deal with it and scoop every day.

Many times, the largest cat is the one most involved with resource guarding. Size seems to matter with cats (it doesn't so much with dogs) and some cats literally throw their weight around. Often, the fat cat is able to intimidate the other cats. Getting cats to lose weight is very difficult, so you are way ahead of the game if you don't let them get fat in the first place. There are really only a couple things you can do to get cats to lose weight; diet is often the hardest, especially if you free feed or have more than one cat. The other option is to get them to exercise more, which can be challenging as they are not dogs and you can't take them for a brisk walk around the block. Use your creative brain and find a game that is irresistible to your individual cat. Don't expect your obese cat to play by himself or with other cats, you have to be involved in his life and actively play with him. You have to be their favorite toy and an emotionally engaged activity director.

Maybe it's a shoe lace, a fuzzy ball, a catnip mouse or a laser pointer, but you must motivate the cat to move. Simple toys are often the best; a feather tied to a string was probably a favorite in ancient Rome. Even lazy swatting is movement and burns calories. Any is better than none. Rotate your toys often. If your animal has a favorite, that one can be out all of the time and two or three others, as well. Every couple of weeks put those toys away and take out some different ones. One of the best cat toys is a laser pointer. A lot of dogs like them, too, especially terriers. A word of caution: Do Not shine the laser in their eyes! I don't recommend lasers for households with young kids. Most animals figure out it is just a dot, but they chase it anyway because it is fun and they get to use their best skills. Use your house as a kitty gym and get the cat to chase the dot up and down the stairs or down the hall. Exercise is essential to all animals (even humans), especially if they need to lose weight.

Scratching is very important to cats and is another great place to draw a boundary. Not only does it sharpen their claws, it exercises the muscles in their feet, legs and back. This is also a way for them to communicate with other animals because they have scent glands on their feet they use to claim their territory. But as soon as claws touch the couch, respond immediately, intensely and predictably. Clap your hands, use some variant of the UN-AC-CEPT-A-BLE tirade (the vocabulary doesn't really matter, but the emotion does) and force the cat to move away from the couch. Do you see how this is more effective than saying something like, "Hey! Quit clawing that! Bad kitty!" and shaking your finger at her?

Make the effort to give a meaningful correction with some real emotion behind it.

Jungle Kitty

It is easier to set a physical boundary with a dog than a cat and your expectation that they stay in the yard is merely a suggestion. It is possible to get cats to be more afraid of cars so that they stay out of the street. Some cats have a thrill seeker personality and like to test their physical abilities. These are the ones that have a lot of problems with cars. They have no way of understanding how fast a car can accelerate and cats always think they can out run it. Some will wait until the absolute last second before they get out of the way. I show them a mental movie about what happens when they get hit by a car, kind of like the movies you watched as a teenager in Driver's Ed. I show them tumbling, getting cut and broken and how painful and scary it is. I let them feel how sad their person would be. I explain to them that cars are stupid, but they can go very, very fast. Then we set some boundaries that exclude the street, sidewalk and driveway (see the section on Moving for a detailed explanation of how to do this). The space inside the boundary is safe and secure and the area outside scary and dangerous. They sometimes disregard this, but often it will encourage them to stay out of the street. This works with dogs as well.

Supervision is very helpful in getting your cat to respect physical boundaries and stay in the area you define. Animals like routine and it is much better for your cat to go outside for ten minutes a day before you feed her breakfast, than to go out for an hour unsupervised now and then. Any cat that is ever outside must be microchipped. Cats are healthier and live longer if they are kept indoors, but some of them are just not happy without some outdoor experience. They really do see themselves as King or Queen of the Jungle. It is your responsibility to meet their needs in a way that will keep them safe. Many times that is the thing we negotiate about, stop peeing on the carpet for some time outside. There are some very clever cat proof fences and I have a client who has a beautifully landscaped back yard with a large cat enclosure (accessed by a catwalk through a window) and a fenced cat tunnel that winds through the shrubs and flower beds. The cats love it. You can try a harness and leash, but you may have a long period of getting the cat to accept wearing it. Your cat is not a dog and they won't really walk with you so be very patient and let the cat dictate the experience. Very few cats like being on a leash.

I control when Monster goes out and I try very hard to keep her from bolting out the door. I physically block her, give her the Game Show Loser noise (a loud "Ernt!" sound) and drop my keys in front of her. She usually tries this when I am distracted and have my hands full. If she gets out, I immediately put down my stuff and give her the command "Get in your house!" and try to direct her back in. Picking her up is a poor option, so I have to convince her to go in on her own. If she refuses, I will use a minimum amount of force. I am a firm believer in the power of annoyance. Very few experiences are truly painful, but many things are annoying enough that I will avoid them. I get a long, thin twig and touch her with it. I don't threaten her or poke her in a way that will hurt her, but I touch her back slowly, rhythmically and as annoyingly as possible. She will growl and try to bite the twig, but then she will storm off in a huff and go in the house. Be creative and compassionate when problem solving with your animals.

Chapter Five: Practical Examples

If you pick up your cat and put him in the house after he escapes, there is no self-determination in that and it is frustrating to him. Visualize what you want to see, give a clear command (*"Getinyourhouse!"* is one word to a cat) and give him the opportunity to choose the right action. Have a little patience and allow him to come in. Monster doesn't get praised for coming in if she bolted because she disrespected a boundary, but she avoids getting reprimanded by coming in voluntarily. I avoid walking around in my robe looking under cars and bushes trying to find her, so this is good for both of us.

Moving

You believe that your home and possessions belong to you. You are wrong. Everything belongs to your animals. In general, animals are very conservative. They like their stuff and they like their routines and they want things to always stay the same. Your home is the center of their universe and moving disrupts it completely. It also brings up their fear of abandonment. Even the idea of moving is stressful for animals. I did a reading for a man whose cat was peeing all over the house and he was about to take the cat to the shelter. One of the other cats told me this cat didn't want to leave the house and I got the emotions of anxiety and abandonment. I asked the man if they were planning on moving. He said he loved the house, but his wife didn't like it and was always threatening to sell it. The cat picked up on this and was claiming his territory the only way he could. I asked the man to have his wife not mention moving for six months so the cat could calm down. I explained to the cat that peeing was unacceptable and made his person very angry. He could stay in his house if he stopped spraying but would be removed if he didn't. He readily agreed and stopped marking.

Moving with animals is where all of your animal communication skills come into play. Sit down in a quiet place with each of them before you start to pack and show them what is going to happen. Look into their eyes and visualize packing everything up, being in transit to your new home and how you will always be together. Add in the feelings of security, love and togetherness. Putting gentle pressure on the **Magic Spot** helps keep them calm because they are not going to like what you are showing them. Play your mental movies early in the process and repeat them often. Emphasize what is in it for them. Do the dogs get a nicer yard? Is the cat going to have more sunny windows to look out? Are the horses going to be near other horses they can visit? Will you be happier and less stressed? If you move to a place that isn't going to be better for your animal, put all of your emphasis on the fact that you will be together, you love them and you will always be there for them.

Moving with animals is not easy, so plan for them before, during and immediately after you move. What is the worst thing that could happen? Your animal gets lost while you are in between two addresses. It can happen and it does. Let your left brain run amok organizing the details of your move. Gather the following items into a kit (for each animal) and keep it accessible at all times until you have physically unloaded everything at your new place. If you fly with your animal, have a copy of this information with you and a copy attached to their carrier. Have the information in multiple languages if appropriate. Put this together long before you start actually moving. Include:

Chapter Five: Practical Examples

- A missing animal flier for each animal. Include your name, your animal's name, phone numbers and email information. This seems obvious, but many people forget to include everything when they make fliers. Include a recent (taken within one month) color photo with only one animal in each photo. Write out a good description, noting any distinctive traits or markings. Include age, weight, sex and breed. If you have a rare or unusual breed, describe it in detail. Have this on paper and in a digital version so you can make copies and start handing them out and post online within minutes.

- Make sure your animal's vaccinations are current and keep proof with you, especially if traveling to another country. If you plan to tranquillize your animal, make the appointment with the vet as early as you can. Keep the written prescription and your vet's contact information available.

- Fill prescriptions for any medication, including things like supplements and ear wipes. Make copies of the labels on the packages. Keep their medications with you and set reminders on your phone so you can keep them on schedule. Use a pill sorter that has compartments for each day.

- If your animal is old or has medical issues, it is a good idea to travel with a copy of their vet records. Have your current vet recommend a clinic in the area you will be moving to and any specialists that your animal may need to see.

- Have a collar on your dog (and your cat, if possible) with current tags. Get a tag made before you leave with your cell phone and a number for someone

- who is not traveling with you. Most pet supply stores have machines that make tags in a few minutes.
- Get contact information for animal shelters and emergency vets at your destination and any place you will be stopping overnight.
- Update your information with your microchip company and give them a cell phone number and the number of a friend or family member they can contact. There is nothing worse than having your animal picked up and they can't get a hold of you. Ask about freezing the information so no one else can change it. Make note of microchip numbers.
- Have more than enough food, water and litter available. Figure out how you will feed them and how your cat will use the litter box while you are in transit. Do not add to your animal's stress by changing their food in the middle of moving because you ran out of what they usually eat. I usually figure on a two-week supply to cover the time before, during and immediately after the move. I like to premeasure the food into individual portions so I don't spill any of it.

Before removing anything from your home, make sure your animals are secure. You don't want your dog biting the movers (it is his stuff after all and he doesn't want anyone messing with it) or the cat disappearing. Shut them in the bathroom and put a note on the door. Cats have been known to get sealed in moving boxes. My parents were moving, had everything out of the house and could not find the cat. She was inside the furnace and had burned off half her whiskers sitting near the pilot light. Please learn from their mistake.

Chapter Five: Practical Examples

Your animal's mental health and physical well-being have to be your highest priority, so know where they are at all times.

Moving is traumatic for your animals. I made a terrible mistake when I moved with Monster. I had been telling her about going to a larger place where she could look out and see birds and silly squirrels. As I was preparing to get on the road, I was running behind schedule, tired and stressed. I took the last load to the truck and I left Monster in an absolutely barren apartment with the two things she hates the most, the vacuum and her carrier. I walked in and she was on top of the refrigerator, yowling. I am always uncomfortable when she is above my head as I could lose an eye if things don't go well. I had to immediately shift my attention away from my *To Do* list and calmly focus on her. I visualized her jumping off the refrigerator and walking into her carrier. Given the alternative of spending another moment in an apartment with only a vacuum in it, she chose the much more positive experience of going with me. My lack of looking at things from her perspective caused her a needless amount of anxiety in an already stressful situation.

Moving is not fun for anyone, especially if your animal is not used to being in a car. Restraints (crates, seatbelts or backseat barriers) are essential to keep your animal safe. They may be quieter if they are not restrained, but I have worked with dogs that have been in accidents and were thrown out of the vehicle. If they weren't seriously injured, they ran as far and fast as they could. Your dog does not need to be sitting on your lap, distracting you while you drive a U-Haul full of all of your possessions with your car in tow. What could possibly go wrong?

If you plan on your dog being in a crate, hopefully you have been practicing setting it up and your dog is comfortable being in it. If you stay overnight someplace during your move, find places that are animal friendly and make reservations early. Even if you have stayed in a hotel many times with your dog or cat without any problems, all bets are off when you move. Everyone is stressed and their behavior can be unpredictable. It can be a very costly mistake leaving a nervous dog alone in a motel room. They can do thousands of dollars of damage and/or hurt themselves in a very short amount of time.

There are also some important steps to take when you reach your destination. Get the animals set up in a room where they won't be disturbed, again the bathroom is good (don't forget the sign on the door). Give them food, water, litter boxes for cats, and some familiar objects like their blanket or toys. They are just as exhausted as you are and the best thing you can do is leave them alone for a while.

Before you turn any animal loose in a new enclosure like a back yard or pasture, you have the responsibility to completely walk the fence and make sure the animal can't get hurt or escape. Some dogs can get through amazingly small spaces, barely larger than their head. Supervise them when you first let them into a new space. As soon as you can, after getting everything in, help them make a visual map of the new area with your house as the center. If they do get out, this can help them recognize where they are and possibly get back to you. Put the dogs on leashes and walk them individually around the house, showing them how to get from the front door to the back door. Then take them down the street two or three houses in each direction, so they have some sense of where they are. Do something similar with cats. Put the cat in a carrier and pretend it is a video camera. Show him the street in each direction and what the front door looks like. Take him around the house and show him good

Chapter Five: Practical Examples

places to hide. Cats are territorial but can easily get chased away if they don't have an escape route or place to retreat.

A lot of people believe that the animal would be able to find its way home to a new house by recognizing your scent. A new house doesn't smell like you for a very long time. If you want to help them out, get some sweaty socks and dirty underwear and rub them on the door frames about a foot up from the ground. Then it really will smell like you. You have effectively scent marked your property in a way they can recognize.

This can also be a great time to create a physical boundary. Put your dog on a leash and walk around the area where you want him to stay. Maybe this is just the front yard, not including the driveway or sidewalk, or the back yard excluding the flower bed. You have to be clear on the boundary you want to create. When the dog looks towards the house or the center of the area, you think, "This is our home, this is where we live now, the center of our universe." Put all the nice, warm, Hallmark-y feelings into that thought. Make it all about positive emotions. Home is safe, secure and the source of everything good. When the dog looks outside this area you think, "Nothing ever happens out there. It is totally boring." Make it emotionally dull and uneventful, like watching paint dry. You want the dog to still be able to go places with you, but his attention should be directed to the house, not anything outside of it.

The point is to make a very large emotional contrast between *Inside*, the area you want the animal to stay in and everything *Outside*. Go around at least three times, following the same path, emphasizing the different emotions. This is especially useful for dogs that are anxious or who have a strong instinct to guard a perimeter (like German Shepherds) because it helps them understand what is important and what they can ignore. Cats are less likely to respect this emotional boundary than dogs but it is still important to do this with them. It is much easier to set this boundary right after you move or when you bring a new animal into your family than trying to correct the behavior after they know what is on the other side of the fence.

Take your cat out in a carrier, but make the area outside your boundary scary so he won't want to explore it. In an apartment, you want the hallway or common areas to be uninteresting. If you take your cat to your apartment in the elevator, show him visually and emotionally that the elevator is a very dangerous thing and he should not go anywhere near it. Visualize it as a mouth that will eat him and make it something to avoid. You don't want the dog to be afraid of the elevator so make it like the car; he can only be in it with you.

Moving is usually a choice and you have time to prepare for it. Being evacuated is a whole different situation. If you live in an area that is prone to some kind of natural or man-made disaster (fire, flood, earthquake, storms, industrial accident...) use your BFHB and have an emergency evacuation plan that includes your animals. The ASPCA has a disaster preparedness checklist on their website as well as a mobile app. Many times in an emergency, people refuse to evacuate or will try to re-enter an area before it is safe because they can't take their animals. If you have warning, you owe it to them to LEAVE EARLY. Your objective is to keep everyone together and take care of their basic needs. Be proactive and have everything on the moving list accessible. Get all of your animals microchipped, just in case. Have enough carriers for all of them and pack food, water and litter in your three-day kit. I always keep these things in my car. How would you transport your large animals? How long does it take you to hitch your trailer and get them loaded? Maybe you should practice. What about feed and water for them? Have an idea where you would evacuate to that allows animals and people to stay together. Your house may have more monetary value, but I have worked with people who have tragically lost animals in disasters and the heartache and guilt stays with them for years. Have a plan and prepare for the worst.

Missing Animals

I don't work with lost animals, but I did when I was starting out. It is not my best skill because I don't see animals as objects in a landscape; I see things from their perspective and receive the emotions they experience. If a cat is hiding in a shed for example, I might see dark and wood, not that she is half a mile North by North East from her house. People's expectations were also unreasonable because they were distraught. They often wanted the animal to show me a street sign so they could go find them. Animals have no idea what street signs are and they can't read.

Usually when cats get out of their familiar territory, they become little wild animals and they hide. They don't move much and you can be five feet from them, holding a can of tuna, calling their name and they won't budge. They usually don't go very far and they don't roam around like dogs do. One thing that can work well is to go out right after sunset and look for them with a flashlight. Shine it into every little space you encounter and look for the reflection from their eyes. If you do locate your cat, you may have to set up a live trap because they tend to stay where they feel protected. Most rescue agencies or humane societies loan them out to people. Cats are smart and you will usually only have one chance with a trap, so practice setting it up and bait it with something they can't grab and run off with.

Some cats don't respond like this. I got two calls about missing cats in one week. One did become wild. His people lived in a rural area and I got the image of him far away from houses or roads, having fun hunting. His chances of survival were slim, but that didn't matter to him, he didn't want to go home. He was lucky because he came up to some neighbors irrigating a field and they brought him back to his people. His person immediately set physical boundaries for him and used treats and praise to teach him to come when called. She showered him with attention and made time to play with him several times a day to help convince him that home was a great place to be.

The other cat was close to her home, but had joined a feral colony. She loved her people, but was much more interested in the companionship of other cats. I asked her if she wanted to go home and got "No." Animals live in the present, and at that moment, she didn't want to be anywhere else. That changed about a month later when she showed up at her family's house after a huge thunderstorm, wet and dirty, but no worse for wear.

Lost dogs behave differently than cats. Dogs will move in an outward spiral and can cover a lot of territory, but may only be a short distance from their home. Dogs tend to wander almost continually. Because they keep moving, it can be hard to sort out where they are when you get conflicting reports of where the dog was seen. Don't assume they have their collar and tags on. Even dogs that are normally friendly often will not come up to someone they don't know, even if that person has food and calls them by name.

One determining factor in animals getting lost is if they are not spayed or neutered. Males will cross danger-

Chapter Five: Practical Examples

ous obstacles like freeways to get to a female in heat. A large percentage of animals that are killed by cars are unneutered males. Intact animals are also stolen by people who want to breed them. Sex drive is a powerful motivator for humans, so it is no surprise that it is for dogs and cats as well. Getting your animal spayed or neutered is an important part of keeping your friend safe, but you also have the obligation to not add to the animal overpopulation epidemic. Several million healthy but unwanted animals are killed in shelters every year.

A woman called me who had lost her dog. After getting her calmed down enough that I could piece together her story, she finally said, "Oh yeah, she was in heat." They lucked out and got the dog back. The same woman called the following year, again because her dog was missing and again it was in heat. She found her dog's body a few hours later; she had been hit by a car. The dog loved her and was very devoted to her, but that was minor compared to her sex drive. Of course she got out of the yard. Maybe the woman should have been responsible and gotten her spayed after she escaped the first time. She didn't. She was planning on breeding her to make back the money that she paid when she bought a purebred dog. I have no doubt she got another dog and repeated the same cycle.

The best way to get a missing animal home is to have already taken action. Be proactive and get them microchipped, even if they "never" go outside. Animals get lost, stolen or separated from their families due to natural disasters every day. Microchips work. In a study quoted by the American Veterinary Medical Association (AVMA), only about 22% of lost dogs that entered animal shelters were reunited with their families. Microchipped dogs were returned to their owners 52% of the time. The numbers are even more dramatic for cats. Fewer than two percent of cats in shelters without microchips made it home, whereas microchipped cats went back to their people almost 40% of the time. For microchipped animals that weren't returned to their owners, most of the time it was due to incorrect owner information (or no owner information) in the microchip registry database. If you adopted an animal from a shelter, have moved or changed your phone number, update your information with the chip company. It literally takes five minutes to do this and it may save your animal's life. Some people object to microchips on principle or think they cause cancer. Nothing is 100% safe 100% of the time. Too much air, water or food can kill you. The benefits of having an animal microchipped far outweigh any potential negatives. This is an example of taking a small action to really help your animal.

Having a missing animal is very stressful and causes people to not think clearly. Focus on getting your animal home, not on how much you miss them. This is very challenging because people experience a lot of fear and anxiety when an animal is missing. Create a mental movie of your friend walking into your home and really feel the relief and joy of their return. Focus on the positive feelings of seeing them in their familiar environment and you hugging and kissing them. This is very difficult, so you will have to do this deliberately with the expectation that you will feel more centered and connected with your animal. Do the **Moving Energy Down and Up Exercise**, the **Breathing Exercise** and anything else that will help you not get overwhelmed by intense emotion. Visualize a golden cord coming out of your heart and going directly to your animal's heart. Send your love to your cat or dog and tell them to follow the cord home

Chapter Five: Practical Examples

to you. It is really important to stay optimistic and not get overwhelmed with negative emotion.

Your left brain excels at making plans and taking action, especially in a crisis. This can totally hijack your strong intuitive connection with your animal. Don't get so caught up doing things like posting flyers or going to the shelter that you overlook the information your animal sends you. Be very sensitive to any impressions or gut feelings that you get. Many times, people have a hunch about where their animal is and it is often correct. Being aware of subtle information in a very emotional situation will test every skill you have developed.

Here are some tips to help get your animal home:

- Call animal control immediately to let them know your animal is missing. Contact your vet and the microchip company to report your dog or cat as missing or stolen. Ask the chip company to freeze your record so nobody else can change the ownership and contact information.
- If you are willing to offer a reward, do so immediately. Be willing to pay that amount within a day of the disappearance and any time after that, even if it takes a year to find your animal.
- Make a flier with a color photo and your contact information on it and hand it to people in the area. It is more effective to go door to door than posting the flier. Ask kids in the neighborhood if they have seen your animal. Begin canvassing right away. Post fliers everywhere you can, but ask permission first. If you post flyers outside, place them in plastic bags, such as Ziploc bags. This will extend the flyers' shelf life.

- Make a digital version of your flier and post it on social media. Immediately post your information on rescue and missing animal websites, including breed-specific rescues.
- Check your neighborhood websites for a *Lost & Found* section. In many communities, this can be located on a radio or TV station website.
- Contact all the shelters and adoption centers in your area and surrounding areas. If the animal is picked up by animal control or turned in, it may end up at a shelter. Go into the shelters and look at the animals if you can. Sometimes they don't describe them accurately. Inquire about other breeds that your dog may be mistaken for. For example, someone may mistake a Scotty for a Miniature Schnauzer.
- Remain hopeful and keep your attention on how happy you will be to see your friend again. Use all of the techniques available to you to keep your energy directed to what you expect, which is your animal returning home.

Hopefully, this section has given you some practical ways to apply your skills. These examples detail the thought process I use to get animals and people working together. The mental preparation steps will give you clarity and help identify how you contribute to your animal's behavior. I encourage you to experiment and be creative in your approach. Many people are able to solve their specific problems using these techniques. You are learning by doing and are creating your path as you go. Just as I had no idea what individual steps were needed to transform Monster into a lovable companion, you are plunging into the unknown with

Chapter Five: Practical Examples

your own animals. The important thing is to keep going. Your journal is your compass. Let it guide you towards more balanced partnerships. The more you practice improving your relationships, the better you will get at it. I know you can do this if you try.

The next section details some of the observations I have made about feeding animals. These are just guidelines, so please consult with your vet about the nutritional needs of your individual animal.

Chapter Six:
Food and Exercise

Feeding your dog or cat is the easiest thing in the world. You go to the store, buy whatever is on sale and dump it into a giant-sized bowl that is never empty, right? Wrong. I have talked to hundreds of people about what they feed their animal and have related that directly to the animal's energy and overall health. Food affects all aspects of your animal's well-being and has a large impact on behavior. Becoming an informed pet food shopper and taking control of what and how you feed them is the best way to give them a long life.

   I was looking at the ingredient list of a food that bills itself as "Healthful" and had pictures of chicken, peas and carrots on the bag. Wheat flour was the first ingredient and chicken was the sixth. Some of the kibble was dyed orange and green to look like vegetables. The good stuff was only on the outside of the bag, not the inside. Most pet food brands available in grocery stores or large pet supply chains are made by huge multinational corporations like Colgate Palmolive, Del Monte and Mars. They are in the pet food business to make money and animal nutrition is often a secondary consideration. Your dog does not know what "Chef Inspired" means and your cat is not impressed by the feline version of an Italian Supermodel on the cat food commercial. Don't believe the marketing hype. Chances are very good that you will find one brand of food and stick with it for the life of your animal. If you are going to feed your dog the same food every day for fifteen years, make sure it is a

Chapter Six: Food and Exercise

good one. Give your animal's food the same scrutiny that you give your own. Read the tiny print on the bag so you know what they are eating.

Your largest expense over the life of your animal is food. I tell people to buy the best food they can afford that is suitable for their animal. That doesn't mean the most costly food. There are plenty of stunningly expensive foods that are basically no different from what you can buy at the grocery store. In a nutshell, look for a food with the fewest ingredients and choose specific ingredients over generic ones. Chicken meal is much more specific than poultry meal, for example. If you don't know what an ingredient is, Google it. There are many websites about pet food and some are pretty militant about what you should or shouldn't feed your animal, so get information from several sources.

Dogs should eat meat and can also eat many other things. Contrary to popular belief, dogs can be vegetarian and some are even vegan. Cats are strict carnivores and must eat meat to get the essential amino acid Taurine. Cats should not be fed dog food and young animals need different nutrition than adults. Ingredients in dog and cat food are listed by weight, so meat (or a specific meat meal) should be one of the first things you see. A lot of food manufacturers will list meat as the first ingredient. This is mostly a marketing gimmick. After it is cooked and processed, there is very little "meat" left. Lamb meal (which has been processed to remove the water) has about four times the amount of protein as lamb meat. When lamb is listed as the first ingredient, it is often little more than a flavoring.

Look for a specific meal in the first three ingredients of the food, like chicken meal, beef meal or herring meal. This should match what is advertised on the front of the bag. If chicken is the first ingredient of a lamb and rice food, don't buy it. The addition of "healthy" foods like carrots, cranberries, kale and things like pre- and probiotics are mostly there to entice you to buy. These additions are based on what is assumed to be healthy for people and are not necessary for dogs and cats. They also drive up the price of the food. One exception is large breed dogs do seem to benefit from the addition of glucosamine and chondroitin in their food. It helps their joints and should be a part of their diet from puppyhood on.

Many dogs and most cats cannot digest grain well, so it should be limited in their diet. Look for a food with the fewest types of grain in it. Some low quality foods will have corn, wheat and rice all listed in the first few ingredients. Grains are less expensive than meat or fat and dry food needs some kind of binder to hold it together. Potatoes and sweet potatoes are carbohydrates that are usually easily digested as are some of the more uncommon grains like barley or millet.

Fat is the most expensive ingredient in pet food. It is an essential nutrient and also improves the taste of the food. Look for a named fat like chicken fat or olive oil instead of something generic like animal fat. Dog or cat food can go rancid pretty quickly, so most have some type of preservatives. Natural preservatives (tocopherols, rosemary oil or vitamin C) are better than chemical preservatives. If you buy a large bag of food, divide it up and store it in airtight containers in a cool place. I put Monster's food into gallon size Ziploc bags and store them in the freezer. Buying the smaller bag may be more expensive, but it may be more economical if you end up throwing out part of a larger bag because it has spoiled. Check the *best-by* date on the bag every time you buy food. Some stores aren't great at rotating their

Chapter Six: Food and Exercise

stock. Don't see an expiration date? Call the company and ask or choose a different brand. There are many excellent smaller manufacturers that sell through independent retailers or online. Take your dog (harder to do with cats) with you to your local mom and pop store and talk to the owners. Most are very knowledgeable and can help you select a good food for your individual animal. Do some research into what type of food is available in your area. If your choices are limited to what is available at the grocery store, make the most informed choice you can. If you are so inclined, go to a dog or cat show and ask people what they feed and why. Some breeds do well on certain foods. The reverse is also true; if you know your neighbor's cat eats cheap grocery store food and it has a horrible coat, chronic ear infections and hideous breath, take that into consideration as well.

Dry cat food comes in an amazing array of shapes and sizes. Some cats will get extremely ritualistic about the appearance of the kibble and will not eat anything else. Dogs seem to be much less interested in food shape, but the size of the kibble can be important. If you have a dog that inhales its food (literally for some giant breeds), larger pieces are better. If you have a dog that eats very fast or is prone to bloat (a very painful and potentially life threatening condition), make an effort to slow down their eating. One trick is to get three or four fist-sized cobbles and put them in the food bowl. Cleaned river rocks work well for this. The dry food will fall between the rocks and your dog will have to eat much more slowly. Some dogs will actually pick the rocks out of their bowl and then eat all the food in one gulp. If this happens, there are specialty bowls that have large protrusions sticking up from the bottom that do the same thing as the rocks. You can also feed the dog on a baking sheet with edges, like a jellyroll pan so the pieces of food are separate. This slows down their eating because they have to eat each piece individually.

Ingredients to Avoid

- **Corn.** Because ingredients are listed by weight, different parts of corn can be listed as different ingredients. If you added up all of the corn ingredients in some cheaper brands of dog food it would be 50% of the food.
- **Partial grains.** These are not even whole grains, these are little bits of grain. They are things like mill run, brewer's rice, de-germed cornmeal or wheat flour. Also ingredients like sorghum and beet pulp are just fiber and have very little nutrient content.
- **By-products.** Essentially by-products are everything that is part of an animal that is not the meat that you would eat. Blood, bone and internal organs are some of the better components. Ingredients in animal food are regulated by The Association of American Feed Control Officials (AAFCO) and there are technical definitions of what those ingredients entail. From their website, "Poultry by-products must consist of non-rendered clean parts of carcasses of slaughtered poultry such as heads, feet, viscera, free from fecal content and foreign matter except in such trace amounts as might occur unavoidably in good factory practice." Yuck. Poultry by-products can come from any type of fowl and the content is always changing, making the ingredient very inconsistent. "Animal by-product meal" is a very scary and low quality ingredient. It is made up of any

kind of mammal that has gone through a rendering plant. Poultry by-product meal would be slightly better; and chicken by-product meal is more specific, but these are all low quality ingredients and should be avoided.

- **BHA, BHT or ethoxyquin.** These are artificial preservatives that may exacerbate allergies and can impact the animal's liver and kidneys. I thought they had been pretty much eliminated from commercial food, but I was looking at some treats and was shocked to see BHA listed right on the package. Read the ingredient panel of *everything* you feed your animal.
- **Sugar, corn syrup, artificial colors, artificial preservatives, salt (sodium chloride).** These are junk food for you and also for your animal. They make the food taste good or look pretty. There is no reason for any pet food to be artificially colored except to make it more appealing to you, the one with the money.

Making Good Choices

Many of the products sold in pet stores to help correct problems are actually only cover-ups for the physical conditions related to poor nutrition. You can buy a myriad of potions to help with: dry coat, itchy skin, excessive shedding, red eyes, ear gunk, bad breath, tarter build up on their teeth, tear stains, gas and loose stools. Or you can feed your animal better food and not have these problems. These are all common symptoms of food sensitivities. People who have a dog that is always itchy will try five different kinds of shampoo before they change their dog's food. When you feed an animal something that it cannot assimilate well, it stresses their immune system and opens the door for all kinds of chronic diseases, like cancer, arthritis or kidney and liver problems. Their bodies are completely overwhelmed by trying to digest food that is essentially poison to them.

Dogs that have food sensitivities are often described as being hyper or having ADD. They can be very difficult to work with because they are unable to focus on what you want them to do. They seem to be in perpetual motion, always into something, always seeking, always moving. They can be obsessive lickers, barkers or diggers. Sometimes they seem like they are half crazy, because they are. Their brains can't work because their bodies are under so much stress. I like a food that is one protein and one carbohydrate. Feeding a simple food is essential if you are trying to determine what ingredient is causing food sensitivities. It is much easier to add another protein or carb instead of sorting through a whole mix to try to figure out what they are reacting to.

There is a lot of controversy about what type of food you should give your animal. Raw and homemade diets are becoming more popular. I have seen some amazing turnarounds in the health of animals that have been fed raw diets. They are not for every animal or every situation, but they can be very useful in some cases, like severe allergies, seizure disorders or genetic weakness. Making your own raw or homemade foods can be expensive and time consuming. Feeding a raw diet is not easy, especially if you travel with your animal. You take on a lot of responsibility and your food handling must be impeccable. If you don't get the right nutrients in the correct proportions, you can cause more harm than good, especially with young animals. Do your research. The Internet is a good source for information, but don't trust the first thing you read. Compare methods and

Chapter Six: Food and Exercise

consult other sources, including your vet. There are some raw diets that are not nutritionally sound, so know what you are getting into.

Dogs have always eaten "people food" and I believe dogs have ethnic diets. The breed that was useful in a certain part of the world would have eaten the same food as the people living there. Arctic breeds like Huskies and Malamutes, for example, do well on a diet that is rich in fish and does not contain grain, chicken or lamb. Dogs whose primary job was to hunt birds, like retrievers, cockers and setters often do well on a food that is poultry based. Breeds who were used to herd sheep would have developed eating lamb and mutton. Dogs bred to move cows may do well on beef. These are generalizations and every animal is different, but looking at what the breed ate historically can help you find a healthy diet for your animal. I do muscle testing to determine specifically which foods an animal is sensitive to. This is a more intuitive technique and one that I will cover in my next book.

If you feed a good quality dry food, you can add people food to your animals' diet, if you do it intentionally. People food is what your great grandmother would have cooked: chemical free meat, complex starches like whole grains or potatoes, fruits and vegetables, with very little sugar or salt added. Just because you eat Twinkies and Doritos doesn't mean your dog should. If you unconsciously feed your dog a slice of processed cheese every time you make a sandwich you will take years off her life. You are adding something to improve their nutrition, not make their food more delicious. Animals don't crave as much variety in their diet as humans do. If you are barbecuing steak or chicken breasts, cook up an extra one for the animals (minus the sauce). Cut it into small pieces (about the size of your thumbnail) and freeze some to use for training treats or to add to their food. Cooked eggs, cottage cheese and vegetables are also good additions. Most packaged treats are pure garbage and some animals get a quarter of their daily calories from treats. This is an excellent place to apply your awareness by limiting the type and number of treats you give your animals.

Many cats love fish. Salmon or mackerel are good choices to add to their diet, but limit tuna; it is too high in magnesium (which can cause kidney and bladder stones). Some cats are intolerant of fish and the problems can show up later in their life. They seem to forget how to be cats. They wander around, meowing all the time or beg for food right after they have eaten, almost like they are senile. Removing all fish from their diet can help the symptoms clear up in a few weeks. The problem is fish is in almost every kind of dry and wet cat food. Sometimes it is obvious, like *Tuna and Salmon Dinner* and other times it is way down the ingredient list and is called menhaden, pollock or haddock. It will take a lot of scrutinizing labels, but there are foods that don't contain fish. Monster is very intolerant of fish (she throws up shortly after eating it) and carefully avoiding it in her diet made a noticeable impact on her behavior. When I first got her, she was agitated all of the time. She would only stop moving for a few minutes to rest and then continued pacing. She never seemed to sleep. Changing her diet helped her calm down enough that she could focus on trying to kill me. I am made of meat, after all.

Changing Their Diet

Anytime you change an animal's food, you need to do it deliberately and with the intent to improve their health, not to save a few dollars. All transitions, even within the same brand should be gradual. Mix ¼ of the new food with ¾ of the old for a couple of days, then ½ and ½ for a couple days, then ¾ and a ¼ before switching entirely to the new food. Use your left brain and treat a diet change like a science experiment. Make careful observations and take good notes. Be objective about this and don't just switch after one bag. They need to be on a new diet for at least six to eight weeks to see an effect. The food the animal likes the best may be the one that is loaded with sugar, salt and low quality ingredients, so be prepared for pushback when you make a change.

If you have an animal that is on a special diet, the other animals in the household are also on that diet, unless there is a good reason why they can't be. If you feed one cat lower calorie food and the others normal food, the one that needs to lose weight will only eat the normal food. There is no reason for him to want to change, so you have to limit the choices for him. If one dog is on a limited ingredient diet and gets special low allergen treats, the other dog gets the same treat. If you give the wrong treat to the wrong dog, you have just undone weeks of diet testing. This will cost more, but do you really have the time and energy to keep track of who gets what treat?

Praise and focused emotion are essential when you need to introduce a new food to your animal. People food, because it is something that we focus on intently, is always fascinating to animals. If you pretend that you are eating and enjoying the new prescription dog food that your dog needs to go on, she will be much more interested in eating it. Pick up the food, imagine that it is delicious and pretend to eat it, with lots of "mmm-mm", "yummy" and lip smacking. Tell the dog how wonderful it is and that you might share some of it with her. Really play up how much you are enjoying the food.

Offer it to her, and then say, "Oh no. It's too good. I can't share with you" and take it away.

By this time, your dog will be completely obsessed with whatever it is you have. Continue your play acting and maybe give her a taste, but only a little. You have to make her want that food more than anything else in the world. Then give it to her and tell her how lucky she is to be eating the yummy food. Praise her like she the best dog on the planet because she is doing what you expected. Again, this is manipulation on your part; you are using your strongest thinking skills against your animal's weakest ones. You are doing this for the best reasons, not to show off how clever you are by outsmarting a dog. The healthiest food in the world is worthless if your dog won't eat it, so do everything you can to get your dog to want this food. This play acting is not as effective with cats, but try it anyway.

How you feed your animals is just as important as what you feed them. It does not mean that you love them less if you take control over when and how much your animals eat. Even if you hate the idea of having any kind of rules and abhor schedules, your animals enjoy routine. They need structure, predictability and clearly defined boundaries. Paradoxically, this gives them freedom, reduces their anxiety and helps them enjoy their life more. Put yourself in your dog's place and see the world through his eyes. Not a lot happens in his day, so mealtime is a Big Deal, something that gives him joy. When you are late feeding him, you are breaking his very reassuring routine and that is stressful. If you realize how important that is to him, you become more committed to making a schedule and sticking with it.

When dishing out portions, use a standard size measuring container, don't guess. A mounded cup has about 20%

more food than a cup only filled to the top. Even a few extra calories a day add up over the course of a year. Don't assume that one cup of food has the same number of calories as one cup of another brand. They can vary widely. Many *Lite* or *Reduced Calorie* foods have almost the same amount of calories as the regular version. Again, read the bag, check the company website and make an informed choice.

If you have always just left a bowl of food out and switch to measured portions and regular feeding times, expect a huge amount of pushback. You have to be prepared for this and committed to the change. A sneaky trick is to start this change when you are out of town and have a pet sitter come in or when you board the animal. That way you don't have to be subject to all of the bad behavior and drama that will take place.

One of the best things I did for my relationship with Monster was to get her an automatic feeder. The one that I have is battery-powered and has five compartments, four of which are covered until the timer goes off, moving the tray to the opening in the feeder lid. It rotates every 12 hours, whether I am home or not. This is our third feeder. She broke the first one and figured out how to reach inside the second one to get food anytime she wanted. My job is to feed the feeder and the feeder feeds her, so I am no longer the subject of her highly focused attention when she is hungry. Monster is not gentle when she wants to be fed. Now if she begs for food (usually about a half hour before the feeder goes off), I completely ignore her. She likes having a very predictable schedule and I like not getting attacked. Use both sides of your brain to really look for a solution to feeding drama.

About half of the animals I work with are overweight and about 20% suffer from food sensitivities. Obesity has the same devastating consequences for animals as it does for people, plus a few more. That extra weight shortens their life and can greatly add to their suffering towards the end. Many animals lose function in their hind legs as they age, partly because being overweight puts pressure on their spine and causes neurological problems. Obesity in animals is almost always the fault of the people doing the feeding, no matter what story they tell themselves.

You are better off not letting them get overweight to begin with. Modify their diet or increase their exercise as soon as you notice them gaining weight. The **Pumpkin Diet** is useful for this. Some unknown genius figured out that dogs will eat canned pumpkin. Even some cats will eat it. Pumpkin is mostly fiber and water and helps animals feel full. Basically, you reduce the amount of food and put in double that amount of pumpkin. Make sure to get a can of Solid Pack Pumpkin, not the Pumpkin Pie Filling that has eggs and spices in it. This is an example of the proportions, adjust the ratio to what you feed.

>   1 cup dry food
>   - ¼ cup dry food
>   --------------------
>   ¾ cup dry food
>   + ½ cup pumpkin
>   ---------------------
>   1 ¼ cup total food

The animal gets more food and fewer calories. This, coupled with daily exercise will help them shed pounds. Pretending to eat and enjoy the pumpkin is a very effective way to introduce it.

The other important part of keeping animals healthy and maximizing the quality of their lives is exercise. Animals

Chapter Six: Food and Exercise

(and people) need to move their bodies every day. If you only take your dog for a five-minute walk twice a week and then go to the park on the weekend to play Frisbee for an hour, his chance of getting injured is quite high. I work with a lot of dogs with hip, back and knee injuries and also see cats with back problems, usually because they have tried to do something that they weren't in shape for. Daily exercise is essential for injury prevention and reducing obesity related problems like diabetes, arthritis and cardiac disease.

As important as exercise is physically, one of the benefits that most impacts your relationship is mental. I worked with two horses who spent 362 days a year standing around the pasture getting fat and three days being ridden into the ground during hunting season. They were both skittish and one was aggressive when they tried to bridle him. Every human interaction was about being forced into extreme physical exertion and they were sore for weeks after. They resented this and had a deep distrust of people. They acted out anytime a person approached. Animals that get regular exercise are just easier to deal with.

Too many dogs, cats and especially horses have behavior problems because they don't get to use their bodies. Animals like to be fit. Exercise gives them a chance to relax and enjoy using their bodies to do the things they are good at like running, jumping or swimming. They are actually tired and will go to sleep instead of getting into trouble. Getting plenty of exercise helps them calm down and focus. For very high energy or young animals, exercising them before a training session can help them better understand what you are asking. You can't get to their brain until you have gotten through their body. Some animals are amazing athletes and are never happier than after they have used their bodies to the fullest. Exercise is like a drug to them and they can't function without it. Many people like to participate in sports with their dogs and horses. This can be a great way to build partnership, meet people of similar interests and get exercise. Other people don't like sports or are not very social, so they have to be more creative in finding ways to exercise their animals.

Because animals get fit faster and stay fit longer than we do, it can be very difficult to keep up with them physically. You owe it to them to at least make an effort. If you can, try to run with your dog at least three times a week. If that's not possible, a good daily walk is essential. The pace of your walk is not dictated by the dog. You should try to get both your heart rate and your dog's elevated. If your dog has poor leash manners, enroll in a basic obedience class and learn how to walk together. If you can't walk your dog, find someone who can. Hire a dog walker or find someone who could run with your dog. Put an ad up at a running store or go to a local race and talk to people. Think your way out of the problem and give your animal the exercise they need.

All animals need exercise on a daily basis and it should be part of your routine with them, but some need a lot less than others. Breed and age are important factors as well as individual needs. If you can, try to match your level of activity with your animal. If you are a couch potato and the very idea of exercising makes you tired, simplify your life and don't choose an athletic dog that needs to run several miles a day. A cat might be a better companion. Some dogs, like Greyhounds, need to run very fast for about two minutes, three times a week. Other dogs need to work much harder to be happy.

Chapter Six: Food and Exercise

Animals seek joy and you can help them achieve that by taking control of their diet and exercise. Even if your dog is old, has eaten bad food and never exercised for his entire life, it is never too late to start. You may not turn him into a marathon runner, but even small changes can have an influence on the quality of his life. These are my personal observations, but I have conversations about food with almost all of my clients. Too many people have never engaged their analytical left brain and evaluated how their choices affect their animal's health. Some animals are very healthy eating grocery store food and others need highly specialized diets. Every animal is different, so use these suggestions to draw your own conclusions about what is right for your unique companion.

Conclusion

Our relationships with animals are great laboratories for experimenting with things like "if...then" thinking and using emotion in controlled ways. The skills and confidence you have developed working with your animals can be expanded into other relationships, even the more challenging ones with humans. Your animals have shown you that you really can ignore your annoying coworker and the value of praising your kid for picking up his room. Creating expectations and setting clear boundaries are skills that are applicable to many areas of your life. I hope you feel empowered to change things for the better.

This book has given you the basic tools to redefine your relationships. You have become a more aware and conscientious partner and your animals truly appreciate your efforts. Don't expect them to send you flowers or a nice card, but know that they are grateful. Take a few minutes to read through your journal and acknowledge the progress you have made, noticing how your attitude about the relationship has changed. Keep building on your success and don't forget to share your joy with your animal.

My next book *Humans Think, Animals Feel, Part 2* will expand on these concepts and introduce you to the more intuitive aspects of animal communication. To illustrate these points, I will share some of the more esoteric lessons they have taught me. Any level of relationship is available to

Conclusion

you and if you never do more than share the feeling of love with your animal, you have improved their life.

Thanks for reading and I hope you enjoy happy and healthy relationships with your animal friends. If you have found it valuable, please share this book with the people involved with animal organizations in your community. I love to do animal communication workshops, events and fundraisers for rescue groups. If you liked this book, take it in to an independent book store and have them order it. Who knows? I might visit your neighborhood.

I would love to talk to you and your animals. Please contact me at *www.pattypetpsychic.com*, where you can schedule a reading, find out about my upcoming classes and watch videos of me working with animals. Be sure and sign up for my newsletter to get animal communication tips, entertaining stories and the occasional discount. You can also follow me on Instagram: *@pattypetpsychic*.

I look forward to hearing from you!

About the Author

Patty Rayman realized at an early age that the pictures in her head were coming from animals sharing their stories with her. The funny thing was, she understood what they were saying.

As a pet psychic, Patty helps people and animals have conversations with each other to improve their relationships. She does readings from photos over the phone, in person through home visits and at events. She especially loves to do fundraisers for rescue groups, because they are her heroes.

Opening the door of communication between humans and animals is the most meaningful part of Patty's life. She admits that to be a good pet psychic takes patience, good emotional boundaries and lint rollers. Lots of lint rollers.

Patty lives in Salt Lake City, Utah with her fat, happy, and (sometimes) charming cat Monster, who is a very demanding editor.

Notes

Notes

www.ingramcontent.com/pod-product-compliance
Lightning Source LLC
LaVergne TN
LVHW051601070426
835507LV00021B/2696